HIGH-TICKET
FOR
AFFILIATE GYMS

HOW TO MAKE AN EXTRA
$100,000 THIS YEAR
BY CREATING AND SELLING A BOLT-ON
TRANSFORMATION PROGRAM

SCOTT CARPENTER

HIGH-TICKET FOR AFFILIATE GYMS:

How To Make An Extra $100,000 This Year By Creating And Selling
A Bolt-On Transformation Program

Scott Carpenter

ISBN:
PT Legends Media
www.ptlegends.com
publishing@ptlegends.com

First Edition

To the entrepreneurs, the risk-takers, the outliers. To the men and women bold enough or just crazy enough to lay it all out on the line and go for it.

The world needs more of you.

ABOUT THE AUTHOR
SCOTT CARPENTER

Scott Carpenter started his first gym in 2012 after saying goodbye forever to the corporate world.

In 2020, he discovered the secret to exploding profitability and impact by bolting on a High-Ticket Transformation program as an additional revenue stream.

He has now scaled his gym business to six locations grossing multiple 7-figures in annual revenue.

The unique system Scott created has generated a huge demand in the gym owner and fitness entrepreneur space.

His company, PT Legends, teaches fitness business owners how to create, sell, and fulfill High-Ticket offers within their unique business models.

TABLE OF CONTENTS

WHY I WROTE THIS BOOK

I knew I was *obligated* to write this book after I received a voice message from a CrossFit gym owner who's been in business for nine years in Louisiana, and whom we had been mentoring and teaching the techniques in this book for just under one month.

It was Tuesday, August 24th, 2021 at 5 p.m. I was in my home office working late on revising some of the training videos we were making for our gym owners.

My phone chimed with the usual tone from Facebook Messenger, slightly different from a text. I threw it a casual glance, and was excited to see that it was Lauren. She had taken a huge gamble working with us—she'd hired and worked with so many mentors and programs over the years, but was still trapped by her business in spite of working her ass off for nearly a decade.

You know the feeling: you keep working harder and harder, spending more money on education, mentorship, continuing education, and leadership. Yet while you may be doing marginally better financially, there still isn't enough money going around to pay other people well so that you don't have to be the CEO, CFO, COO, Marketing Director, Ads Manager, R&D Lead, Staff Manager, Babysitter, Coach, Recruiter, Nutrition Coach, Only Person Who Reaches Out to Old Clients, Punching Bag for Shitty Members' Complaints, and maybe even Floor & Bathroom Cleaner.

Lauren was supremely talented, incredibly hardworking, and had invested in herself and in her business over the years. But the stress, the setbacks, the ever-present 50+ hour work weeks with no relief in sight, and the feeling of being trapped by her business were taking their toll. When we first spoke, four weeks earlier, I could feel the pain the past nine years of operating her business had taken on her, her husband, their relationship, their health, and their children.

"I can't keep doing this…" she said, holding back her tears. "I've tried everything. I've hired so many mentors and spent so much money. This has to be it. I just can't keep going on like this."

My heart bled.

I know that pain. Several years ago I had two gyms that completely melted down—the first because the person I trusted the most ended up having sexual relations with a subordinate female trainer, then denied and attempted to cover it up until it caused a mutiny among the entire staff. The entire business melted down as employees quit and the place completely fell apart.

But instead of firing him—since I thought he was fundamentally a good person who, because of personal hardships, had made some bad decisions—I gave him a second chance. I relocated him to the other gym I owned and was currently working in.

And, as you can probably guess, that was a stupid move. He did it again. He abused his position and hooked up with another female coach. In a matter of months, almost all the staff from both locations left. And yes, one of the former coaches even became a competitor and opened up a business, with cheaper rates, taking my clients, just a few blocks away.

So after I finally fired the guy who started all the trouble, I was left with two locations that had imploded, hardly any staff, and long-term personal guarantees on the leases which would spell bankruptcy. To make matters worse, I was constantly fearing two lawsuits. One, if my business would be named in a sexual harassment lawsuit against the offender. The second was unexpected. I was tipped off by a former client that the guy who started all of this hell was going to sue *me*.

The gall of that guy. Of course, it gets worse. After he left was when I found out that he'd also stolen over twenty thousand dollars by making side arrangements. I learned, too, that he'd been sending dick pics on the regular (are you really surprised?). And now he was suing *me* to try to get a handout.

I worked 60-80 hours per week, going in to take 4-a.m.'s and finishing past 8 p.m. I was working Saturdays and Sundays. Over and over, week after week, month after month, trying to recover the bottom line and get the bills paid.

I had no other choice; at the time, I had a newborn son, a girlfriend to make my wife, a mortgage, a car payment, and previous little savings. And every day I would check the mail with utter dread that there would be a letter from an attorney about a lawsuit. The fear, stress, and desperation were present every single hour of every single day.

I didn't even have time to think about how long I could keep up with this unsustainable work, stress, and schedule. I was far too busy trying to keep my head above water.

Thankfully, this story has a happy ending. With grit and a fair amount of luck, I was able to turn things around with the help of some amazing staff members (who are now partners). Currently, the six gyms I operate bring in millions each year, and my time today is spent helping other gym owners around the world implement the High-Ticket secrets I'm sharing with you in this book.

So yes—When Lauren gave me her story and shared her pain and desperation, I *felt* it. I know firsthand the desperation of feeling trapped by your business with no clear way to get out of working those long hours.

It was my responsibility to do everything I could to help Lauren. But she had her doubts about starting and working with me and the team at PT Legends. Even though we were connected through another gym owner she trusted who saw amazing results with us, it was still scary to spend money on hiring yet another business coach.

Her CrossFit group rates averaged $129 per month, had a bit of one-on-one private training, and offered nutrition coaching at $99 per month. (Not bad, but the number of hours she was servicing was terribly high. And, with low rates, it wasn't economically feasible to have someone else do the work, particularly with low renewal rates.)

In her small town, she, rightfully, had doubts that anyone would or could pay $2,000, $3,000, or $5,000 for a 9-12 week program.

She had to overcome that doubt, plus learn and develop the confidence that she, and her services, were worth that kind of money.

Within the first week of working with me, Lauren sold her first High-Ticket Transformation program, which was a group CrossFit 3 times per week with a weekly 20-30 minute Coaching Session:

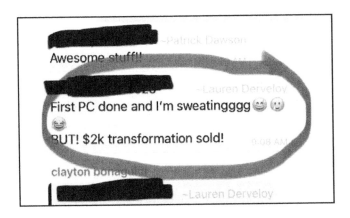

And, just a couple days after:

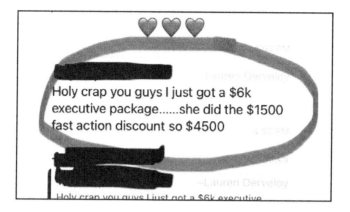

By the end of the first four weeks of us working together, Lauren sold $19,500 in new business from only a small handful of leads—something that would have been utterly *impossible* had she not added a High-Ticket offer.

She would have had to sell 73 memberships, or 95 nutrition coaching add-ons, to achieve that amount of revenue per month. And who on earth has that many warm leads coming in to their business to make that happen?

Instead, she did it by closing six Perfect Consultations. Six new clients. That's it.

So back to my cozy home office on Tuesday, August 21st. I was working late creating more training content for other gym owners we'd begun working with. I knew what we were doing was important, but when Lauren's voice message came through on my Facebook Messenger, it changed everything for me.

Immediately she began choking up, and I couldn't help it, either.

"It's so important for me to just thank you guys so much. I'm super emotional right now because... in nine years of business, I've never, I've *never* felt this type of freedom...

And it's just really important for me to say thank you, because I can truly say that for the first time in nine years… *I feel free.*"

It wasn't so much what she said; it was the *way* she said it. You could feel the relief in her voice. The weight of feeling trapped and enslaved by her business, the toll it had taken on her family and self-worth—you could hear it all leaving her body. That was the moment when this became something else, something bigger.

Now I knew there was no turning back; this was something I *had* to do. I couldn't simply just take on a gym owner or two if I felt like it.

This is something I *have* to do because there is no other choice. There are so many other gym owners who are struggling in the same way. You may be one of them, whether you're just getting by and making ends meet, or you're doing well but can't seem to break through the plateau and realize your true potential.

So that's why I wrote this book, and that's why it's my mission to get a copy in every CrossFit owner's hands.

You started your business because you wanted freedom and control of your destiny, and to make an impact in others' lives.

I will teach you how to bolt on a High-Ticket Transformation, without changing your business model, to have the freedom of time, money, and impact that you desire from your business.

I want to help you make an extra $100,000 this year. Are you ready? Let's go!

Scott Carpenter

WHY THIS WILL WORK FOR YOU

In High-Ticket For Affiliate Gyms, I'm going to teach you how to create a High-Ticket Offer within your gym, without changing your business model at all, and keep the process nice and simple.

Most business books are bloated with an extra 100 pages of fluff. If you're a gym owner, you are busy. My intention is to skip the fluff, shave off the unnecessary pages, and give you only the good stuff.

Regardless of where your CrossFit is located, your current rates, or the demographics of your city or town, this *will* work for you. I know this for a fact because this 100% works for gym owner clients we have in poorer areas in Mississippi, Louisiana, Kansas City, Ireland—all over the US and the rest of the world. They all charge at least $2,000 to $8,000 for their High-Ticket Transformation Programs.

This is the system that completely changed my business in an incredibly short period of time, and has also done so for dozens of other CrossFit gym owners. The crazy thing is—I've never even owned a CrossFit gym. If you told me three years ago that I'd be helping affiliates lead movements and achieve financial freedom, I wouldn't have believed you.

But rest assured, I have 14 years of experience in the industry as an employee and multiple business owner, and my studios bring in multiple 7-figures in revenue.

I started working in the industry with Life Time Fitness for four years as a personal trainer, assistant department head, and then as a department head with 25-30 trainers on staff. I couldn't contain my entrepreneurial spirit and naively bought a failing group training studio in Phoenix, Arizona in 2012.

I brought one-on-one personal training into the business model, and eventually semi-private training as well. I struggled for the first few years as I grew to multiple locations *way* before I was ready for them. But my ignorance and stupidity actually ended up being assets in the long run, because I was too stubborn and too proud to fail.

I made every mistake in the book over the years, and I undoubtedly invented new ones.

After some time, I began to do pretty well in the business. I had a handful of locations, and minority partners as owner-operators in some of them.

Business was good, and over time I was able to become functionally retired. I could run the business in under five hours per week from my home, but I found myself bored, uninspired, and feeling lost. I lacked purpose and drive. While my business was good, it turned out that *good* was holding me back from becoming *great*.

In 2020, everything changed. My partner, Dave Bess, had just lost three of his main guys at the Arrowhead studio.

And then—the Covid pandemic hit.

If you remember the early days, it was an extremely fearful time. The government was treating our gyms like they were the sole spreaders of the virus and shutting them down—in many cases, indefinitely. The fear of the unknown, especially not having any idea of when we'd be able to reopen, was horrible to gym owners across the world.

On top of all this, Dave just had his firstborn son as the gyms were officially closed down and revenue took a nose dive. The panic set in, and he feared for his family.

While Dave had paid for expensive coaches and mentors to try and crack the nut in the online training space for a few months prior, the panic drove him to put $10,000 more on a credit card to work with yet another new coach. Like for most fitness professionals, the desperation to figure out and monetize online training became priority one, two, and three.

On March 26th, Dave and I met at our Desert Ridge location. I remember it clearly. Dave was scared, and was brave enough to show it. He cried. I remained calm and collected, so that I might give him some sense of assurance that we would get through this. But inside, I was gutted. As the leader of this organization, I felt 100% responsible for the way he was feeling. I felt like I had let him down.

But we sat and mapped out online strategies, price points, and a plan moving forward. The problem was that it was exactly what everyone else was doing. It was low-priced and affordable, and absolutely not scalable. The math didn't check out. Without a reasonable price point, the cost of acquisition was too high and average membership length of a client too short. There was no possible way we could be successful with this. The math simply didn't check out.

We dumped more money hiring different coaches and taking different courses. The tens of thousands of dollars were adding up, but we began to learn from high-ticket coaches and programs and discovering the power of a high price point and the magic of selling it.

Between the two of us, we spent over $80,000 during a very short period with different coaches, programs, and masterminds. And while we learned a lot from them, none of the programs were really designed to be built into the brick-and-mortar space.

And no gym-based coaches were teaching techniques on how to charge $74 for classes or $111 for semi-private training sessions.

So, what we did was take a smattering of the teaching from all these different programs, and merged it with an amazing, turn-key coaching system I had developed and piloted with amazing success (more on this later).

Thankfully, our gyms were in a reasonable pandemic response state, Arizona. We were able to open up again after a few months and get back to work, and we began to apply this system to our brick-and-mortar gyms.

We launched this entirely new High-Ticket Transformation program in Dave's Arrowhead location in August of 2020. Within the first four weeks, Dave sold $40,670 in new business alone (9-week programs, 3 times per week semi-private sessions).

It felt *amazing*. More than amazing. I hadn't been this excited since I started the business back in 2012.

We could see how this could change *everything*. All we had to do is bolt-on the same system to all the other locations.

But you have to realize something: Dave is *amazing* at sales (I call him the Kool-Aid Man—after getting off of a call with him, you'll feel like you run through brick walls). He can easily sell this. But selling High-Ticket is a different matter. Is this scalable? Could we teach our other gym operators how to make this system work?

The answer is: **hell yes**.

We successfully taught and implemented this program across all our gyms in the valley, and every single one of them hit all-time revenue records within months, even in the heart of Covid-19 with less-than-ideal lead flow. My staff, consisting of both veterans and rookies, picked this system up quickly and crushed it.

A TYPICAL MONTH OF NEW BUSINESS REVENUE AT MY GYMS

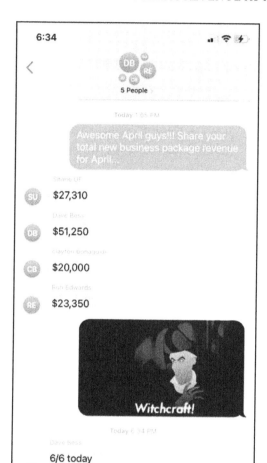

Things were looking incredible. The world was shrinking at the time but we were growing like never before.

A year or two prior, I had joined a mentoring group for CrossFit gym owners. While I wasn't an affiliate gym, I enjoyed being part of a group of other gym owners, as well as having a coach to meet with on a monthly basis. It was a great experience. I encourage all gym owners who are going solo to find a group—it makes a huge difference.

As I shared the development and results of adding our High-Ticket Transformation offer into our business, other CrossFit gym owners took notice. After all, the results were stunning. You know, the almost too-good-to-be-true numbers that you think are either made up or so crazy you don't believe you'd be able to duplicate them at your gym.

The gym owners wanted to ask some questions about what we were doing, so we hopped on a Zoom call and I showed them.

"So can you teach me how to do this in my business?" was all they asked.

At first I wasn't so sure. While it was originally designed for my personal training and semi-private training business model, we hadn't tested the system on group models. But I was riding a big high. All of my problems—the fear of losing one or two key employees and having to jump right back into working 40 hours a week in a location, the fear of not having enough leads, the fear of "what if"—went away when we brought in High-Ticket.

It would be selfish of me to keep a secret this good to myself, so Dave and I agreed to teach it to these gym owners. We got to work on modifying it specifically for CrossFit gyms.

And…

The CrossFit boxes blew up! Knocked the doors down in their businesses. They shattered what they knew was possible for their businesses, and the entire trajectory of their lives, in just 4-8 weeks.

And you can guess what happened next: they told their other CrossFit owner friends.

And then they called us. And then they blew up. Then they referred their gym owner friends.

So, we ended up having to build out trainings, portals, weekly Zoom training sessions, coaching materials, software, the works. That's how PT Legends was born. And while we never dropped a dollar into marketing our business, it began to grow by leaps and bounds solely because of the results we were getting gym owners, and therefore solely from word of mouth, gym owner to gym owner.

The funny thing is, we never set out to build this business. It was completely by accident.

And yes, while our CrossFit gym owners are all making far more money, while working less in the business, the best part is that they are having *fun* again. For the first time in years, business has become rewarding and *exciting*. As it has for me as well—I have truly found my purpose.

Our goal is to teach each and every CrossFit gym owner, who wants to have a bigger impact in others' lives and their communities, who wants to be the leader of a movement, how to make that dream a reality.

The money and financial freedom is just icing on the cake.

This system works. What I'm about to share with you in this book is easily worth $100,000. I'm not going to hold back the good stuff; I'm not going to say, "You need to work with me through PT Legends if you want the real answers." You're going to get them all here.

Now, after reading this book, many of you will choose to work with me. If you do, and you put in the effort, your business and your life will forever be changed. You'll see the stories of Legends sprinkled throughout this book and their results.

It's great if you work with me. Helping gym owners win gives me more satisfaction than anything else I've done in life. That's probably because I know how hard, stressful, lonely, and scary being a gym owner can be. I've made it through to the other side, and I want to bring along as many as I can with me.

But if you choose not to, I urge you to take action on the strategies in this book. Everything you need to make an extra $100,000 this year is within these pages. Life is too short not to go for it.

But enough story time; I promised I'd cut to the chase and dig right into it.

You've got 101 things to do—let's get to the good shit.

SHANNON LOGAN

Gym:

TRUE CORE

LOCATION: Annapolis, MD

IN BUSINESS FOR: 7.5 years

BEFORE PT LEGENDS & HIGH-TICKET:

We were stuck at a revenue plateau. We couldn't break through a certain mark, and even though I kept trying to increase our product offerings, or improve our sales metrics, nothing seemed to work. It was as if we were at a ceiling and all the other business advice I was getting was not working.

AFTER PT LEGENDS & HIGH-TICKET:

We surpassed our previous gross revenue best by 140%!!! My coaches are making more money than they ever have—while working LESS hours. I am not chasing the number of intro appointments any longer. Instead, I look forward to having quality, meaningful conversations with prospects and really learning the best way to help them.

Everything I had previously thought about sales has changed. I now have the confidence and belief in myself to sell packages over 10x what we were previously charging. It has given me the ability to see that freedom of time is really possible for me and my family.

AMAZING HIGHLIGHTS:

$7000 9-week VIRTUAL coaching program

140% increase in gross revenue.

.

CHAPTER 1

GET UNSTUCK AND UNFUCKED

"Don't worry, I'm not gonna do what you all think I'm gonna do,
which is, you know... flip out!"
— *Jerry Maguire, Jerry Maguire*

There are two types of CrossFit owners. You are either:

1. Struggling. You're working a lot of hours, but taking home meager pay. Maybe enough to cover the bills, but not enough to have real security and financial peace of mind to pay for you, your family, college funds, retirement, and vacations. Eventually, if not now, you will be wondering if you can keep doing this for the next ten years—and you may be secretly wishing someone would just offer you a secure, high-salary job to leave it all behind.

or...

2. Doing Pretty Well, but bumping up against a glass ceiling. You're making $80-$150k, maybe even a bit more, and you've tried many things to get past that level. You've hired coaches, bought programs, and improved things, but you're running into difficulties improving your revenue past a certain amount—particularly without you as the business owner putting in the majority of the effort. You keep working harder and harder to improve

the business, but the gains get smaller and smaller. While most owners would kill to be in your position, you find yourself getting bored, and perhaps a bit lost as to what to do next.

I personally was a 1) Struggling Owner for many years before I began to do well. But, oddly enough, my experience wasn't much different when I went on to 2) Doing Pretty Well.

In both cases, I felt hopelessly trapped by my business…

Back when I started my fitness businesses, I was filled with hopes and dreams of what I wanted my business to be and how it would enrich my life, my employees' lives, and my clients' lives.

Maybe like me, you too couldn't wait to be the leader of a movement. You envisioned yourself as a pillar of wisdom and motivational force who others would look up to; as a result of heeding your advice, their lives would be healthier, fuller, and better.

People in the community would respect you, give rave reviews, and credit you with changing their lives.

It's a great vision…

But then—reality sets in.

Small business is *fucking tough.* Tough as shit.

You realize that 90-95% of people don't listen to a word you have to say about nutrition. But even so, they're happy to let you and everyone else know that they're not losing any weight—that maybe they need to be doing something else for workouts.

They'll also demand more class times, complain about other group members, want to do their own thing, ask for holds, start again but not be committed to changing anything other than coming in to your gym 3x/ week.

Many of them don't value what you do. And that's frustrating, because you probably got into this business because fitness made a huge impact in the quality of your life—and you really want it to be that impactful for everyone else.

In reality, only 5-10% of clients actually see a true transformation, where they'll say, "Matt really gave me a second lease on life. Coming to Valley CrossFit changed my life."

Think about that for a second. Even in spite of your best efforts, doesn't your business fall within that range?

But the thing is, just a small handful of clients who see those life-changing results makes all of your struggles and hardships worth it in the end.

It makes the 4-a.m.'s and the 8-p.m.'s and the Saturdays and the occasional Sundays worth it.

Let's not deny, though, that the majority of your people really don't value you or your business as the expert and authority like they should.

In short, you aren't making the *impact* that you want in the world. You aren't changing lives like you envisioned. But what if instead of 5-10% of your clients achieving that life-changing transformation—what if that was 70-80% of your people?

What if you worked with a smaller number of clients, who paid 10x more, valued you as a professional, listened to everything you said, and truly transformed their lives? What if you only worked with your dream clients? How much more rewarding would that make your days?

But let's not forget what can be the hardest part of owning a small business: money and risk. The vast majority of CrossFit owners aren't making enough money to provide financial security, let alone abundance, for themselves, their family, or their employees.

This is perhaps the scariest part.

I've been there. I remember that intense feeling of desperation—the stress of paying rent, utilities, payroll, financing payments…

And most of us have personal guarantees on the lease. If things don't work out, we're fucked. The landlord is coming after our personal assets, and they'll win.

You *cannot* be a martyr. Don't give yourself the excuse that you don't do it for the money, that you do it because you love it.

That may be true, but it's also a cop-out. Face it: you are giving yourself a built-in excuse to not be successful. And be real with yourself: you want to make great money. You may not desire to drive an $80,000 car, but you do want to have the means to hire others to take on different roles in your business, as well as money in the bank to breathe.

It is your responsibility, your duty, to be wildly financially successful. Not just to yourself, but also to your family, your employees, and your clients.

You owe it to yourself because you've taken on huge amounts of risk and responsibility, and risk needs to be rewarded.

You owe it to your family, because you need to be an example for what is possible in life if you dedicate yourself to constant improvement—and you also desire to give your family the best opportunities and experiences in life.

You owe it to your staff, because they deserve to be able to make a great living within your business. If your box isn't charging enough, if the margins are too thin, you cannot afford to pay them a reasonable wage. You know you want to give them a rewarding career. What good is your business if you are the only one who makes a decent paycheck?

And finally, you owe it to your clients to charge a premium price and be successful. I know that sounds strange, that it is to their benefit that you charge a high price.

On the surface, it's easy to see. If you aren't financially successful, you'll close and now you can't help anyone. You'll be forced to close not only if you can't pay the bills, but also if you continue doing all the work yourself, and not delegating tasks that you don't enjoy to employees or hiring companies to do work that you suck at. Do you feel burned out now? If your business isn't financially successful enough to pay for roles you don't want to do, you will be. And if you burn out for too long, you'll either find a way out of your business, or you'll resign yourself to being trapped.

But it's also important to your clients to charge a lot of money for their success. If you're talking to a client, and you're charging anywhere from $129 to a few hundred dollars a month to start, they'll think, "Sure, I'll give it a shot." It's just not enough money, not a big enough sacrifice, for them to take it seriously.

But when you charge $3,000 for a 9-week high-ticket Transformation program, you have their full, undivided attention. They have skin in the game. They are invested. They are forced to bet on themselves and take it seriously.

PEOPLE WHO PAY, PAY ATTENTION.

So, don't lie to yourself by saying, "Money isn't that important to me." Because guess what? It isn't just about you. You have a greater responsibility to others, not just yourself.

Of course, money isn't everything. You need the *time* to enjoy it as well.

Does the thought of taking a vacation for one week—without answering any emails, texts, or correspondence with your business—terrify you? Have you actually done this anytime in the past several years? What about for two weeks?

If you feel like you can't get away from your business, or you can't seem to enjoy your time away because you're worried that everything will fall apart, this a problem that will take a toll over time.

You want to own a business, not a job. You need to build your business that serves you and allows you to live the life you want to live.

If you're not there yet, you probably feel like the business owns you, or that you are at its mercy. Maybe physically, maybe psychologically. But if you're stuck, if you feel burnt out, if you feel like you're lost, read on.

The coming chapters will help you get unstuck. You'll learn how to un-fuck your business by adding a High-Ticket offer to create an abundance of time, money, purpose, and impact.

Not only can you turn around your business in 4-8 weeks, it will also *be fun* again. Operating a business can become a stale grind after years.

This will change everything. Read on.

DAVID OQUENDO

Gym:

MAXIMIZE LIFE FITNESS AND NUTRITION

LOCATION: Kansas City, MO

IN BUSINESS FOR: 6.5 years

BEFORE PT LEGENDS & HIGH-TICKET:

I really wanted to provide a good living not just for me but also for my employees. I wanted them to be able to have a sustainable career. This wasn't a possibility charging the market rates that I was currently charging—the margin just wasn't there to pay people how I wanted to pay them.

AFTER PT LEGENDS & HIGH-TICKET:

Definitely the confidence to sell high-ticket packages and the confidence to actually have a program that does more than fitness.

PT Legends is the reason we changed our trajectory. It's been a total game changer. It pushed us out of our comfort zone and it's seriously set us up to do amazing things.

AMAZING HIGHLIGHTS:

Honestly, having the confidence to sell multiple thousand-dollar packages without blinking. That is the biggest thing that has impacted us.

We sold over $20,000 in new business in the first month of execution!

SCOTT CARPENTER

CHAPTER 2
THE MATH DOESN'T ADD UP

"They've done studies, you know. 60% of the time, it works every time."
— *Brian Fantana, Anchorman*

If you've made it this far in the book, chances are your monthly revenue isn't where you want it to be. You want to grow.

But you know how hard it is past a certain point. You end up working harder and harder for smaller and smaller gains, breadcrumbs really. And when you take your foot off the gas, your revenues fall back to that natural range they tend to settle into.

This probably looks familiar to you…

Unfortunately, your limited business model has created this problem. When you only have commodity-priced, $99 to mid-$200's monthly group memberships, it's extremely hard to get around this problem.

The math taps you out—it just doesn't add up.

Depending on which self-reported industry surveys you look at, the median cost for unlimited group memberships is $118 to $159 per month.

Let's use $150 for some easy math.

$150 x 150 members = $22,500 / month.

Once you figure in rent, utilities, software, processing fees, staff costs, maintenance, and all the odds and ends—you aren't looking too hot here.

Let's say you work your ass off, you've hired some business mentors, taken some courses, run some ads, improved your sales, refined your operations, and added value to increase your retention. Now you're up to 200 members.

$150 x 200 members = $30,000 / month

Now, depending on factors such as your population density, competition, and others, your numbers may be naturally higher or lower than 150-200.

At 200 members, you're doing much better, but your costs are also rising—and you're more likely looking at a larger space and more overhead.

But why is it so damn hard to move past a certain number of memberships?

It's just math.

It's because your churn (how many members you lose each month), works harder and harder to erase your gains the more successful you get.

If you have 150 members, and you lose 8% of your clients each month, you need to sign up 12 members just to prevent yourself from sliding backwards!

The better you do, the harder it gets! If you have 200 members, you need to sign up 16 members just to maintain where you're at.

And at 250, you're looking at losing 20 members per month. Your churn may be lower, but don't kid yourself—you have to count everything: the ones who leave after the first month, the holds, the "exceptions," etc. I happen to be using kind numbers; the industry average is over 11%.

Unless you happen to be lucky enough to have a location that's a never-ending organic lead factory, this is the reason why you're struggling so damn much!

And, unfortunately, getting leads has become harder and harder to do. Even before the pandemic, the cost of online advertising had skyrocketed over the past several years. And once Covid hit, big money started flowing into the advertising space, driving the cost per lead even higher.

In addition, the effectiveness of ads went way down. If you've ever run Facebook ads, I'm sure you know the giant shit show that can be—50% of people ghost you and never respond, 10% are pissed off you contacted them, 15% think you're giving something away for free, and half of the ones you do book end up either no-showing or leaving after a month anyways.

The pandemic sure hasn't helped. Most CrossFit gyms that rely on heavy volume for large group, with very little to no personal training or semi-private training, are having the hardest time reaching pre-Covid numbers. Depending on your country, state, province, or city lockdowns, you probably saw cancellations by the dozens. How long will it take you acquire and hold on to another 50 members?

Another strategy CrossFit gyms use is to add more services—boot camp classes, kids' classes, senior classes, spin or yoga classes, and everything else. They may add some marginal gains, but after all the effort of marketing these, the added confusion of memberships and options, and the management of additional employees or contractors… is it worth it?

And to do all that, you're going to need thousands of additional square feet in expensive commercial real estate. Most gyms I know need far less space than they have, and could be saving thousands on rent and utilities.

As I'm writing this, I just got off of a call with a CrossFit owner who is doing well, $50,000 to $60,000 a month, but he's managing over 20 people on staff to take care of that—not to mention the drama and constant complaints that come with stocking his gym full of low-paying clients. He would love to grow to multiple locations, but this doesn't scale AT ALL. Despite his best efforts, maintaining his group numbers is a battle he's been losing. His High-Ticket Offer, on the other hand, averaged $15,000 to $20,000 a month over his first 2.5 months after working with me in PT Legends.

UNPOPULAR TRUTH: GETTING MORE CLIENTS AT LOW PRICES WILL TAP YOU OUT. THE MATH DOESN'T ADD UP.

Other business coaches will preach that you need to focus on member retention. And they're right—except for the fact that you are now choosing to focus on something that will give you diminishing returns.

Of course, you need to provide great service. You need to dial in your fulfillment to keep your people engaged. But you can only get your churn so close to zero.

I don't need to spell this out for you; you know this by looking at your own experience. No matter how good of a job you do, how much you care, or how much effort you or your staff put into your service, people will always quit.

They'll get promoted and move to a different area or state, they'll get sick and have health issues, they'll get in an accident or face injuries and surgeries, they'll lose interest and get bored, or they'll have legitimate financial issues.

UNPOPULAR TRUTH:
YOU CAN ONLY DO SO MUCH FOR RETENTION—
A LARGE PART OF IT IS OUTSIDE OF YOUR CONTROL.
YOU CANNOT WIN BY PLAYING DEFENSE.

There is really only one way off of this hamster wheel. There is a wild card you can play that will wildly tilt the scale of success in your favor.

You may have already caught on:

You don't have a lead problem.

You don't have a retention problem.

You have a PRICING problem.

Your pricing model is broken. The math just doesn't add up.

You, my friend, need a High-Ticket Offer!

Let's break down the math and see how adding a High-Ticket Offer will change your business over the next twelve months. For simplicity's sake, we'll just compare apples to apples and look at a standard 3x/week CrossFit group membership versus the same 3x/week CrossFit group Transformation Program.

Now, you may have onboarding programs that change the math a bit, and there are many upsells and downsells available to you, but let's just take a simple look at a few simple scenarios:

SCENARIO A:

With a typical CrossFit model, let's say this month you sit down with 10 Consults, you're a sales killer and close 80% (a couple of your leads were garbage), and you add 8 clients at $155 per month each. That's $1,240 per month.

After 12 months with 10% churn (you lose 10% of your new business added each month), you'll look like this at month 12:

New Client Revenue at Month 12: $1,240

Recurring Client Revenue at Month 12: $7,761

Total Revenue at Month 12: $9,001

Total Revenue Over 12 Months: $70,585

This is just an illustration on new business. The reason your business stops growing is because your churn is based on your total client load, making it so damn hard to break past plateaus!

Now, compare this to a High-Ticket Model.

SCENARIO B:

We're going to give you the same closing rate, 80%. But now you have bolted on a High-Ticket offer for those who have a real problem to solve, need more than just workouts to get there, and are ready to make a real change. If 75% of your new clients sign up for group, and 25% of your new clients sign up for High-Ticket, you'll add 6 group members and 2 High-Ticket clients each month.

Out of these 2 High-Ticket sales, you sell one Transformation (group option) at $2,000 and one Accelerator (PT option) at $3,000 for these 9-week programs.

For easy math and an apples-to-apples comparison, we'll convert this to a monthly rate of $963 and $1,444 respectively.

After 12 months with 10% churn (you lose 10% of your new business added each month), you'll look like this at month 12:

New Client Revenue at Month 12: $5,930

Recurring Client Revenue at Month 12: $37,100

Total Revenue at Month 12: $43,030

Total Revenue Over 12 Months: $337,466

That's a 478% increase just by selling two High-Ticket programs a month! You're looking at well over $22,000 in extra revenue every month for 12 months! Without bringing in any more leads or changing anything in your business model—just by simply bolting on an additional option for those who need more than workouts.

Is an extra $267,000 this year worth your time to learn this system? Can you afford not to?

SCENARIO C:

You may be thinking: there's no way that churn would be the same with a high-ticket option. That's actually a HUGE MYTH; I'll get to that in the later chapters. But, let's say we DOUBLE your churn to 20% in this scenario, not only for your two monthly High-Ticket clients, but also for your regular group clients! This means any new client, High-Ticket or not, would only stay a measly five months.

New Client Revenue at Month 12: $5,930

Recurring Client Revenue at Month 12: $21,979

Total Revenue at Month 12: $27,909

Total Revenue Over 12 Months: $256,671

That's still a 364% increase, $15,507 extra per month, or $186,000 per year improvement!

This is the power of high prices.

This is the only way the math works out for you.

You can grind, month after month, and fool yourself into thinking that you can get there.

Or, you can bolt-on a High-Ticket option for those who need it—and change your life by selling just one to two per month. And if you're selling five to six or more, like many of our Legends do, buckle up because your life is about to immensely improve no matter how your business is currently doing.

This is the only way to drastically move the needle in a short period of time.

Are you willing to give this a shot?

Then read on.

FEATURED LEGEND

TREVOR WARNKE

Gym:

GAME CHANGING PERFORMANCE

LOCATION: Mundelein, IL

IN BUSINESS FOR: 8 years

BEFORE PT LEGENDS & HIGH-TICKET:

We wanted to increase our overall ARM per member but knew that just adding items that have a COGS wouldn't make the jumps we needed.

We were doing nutrition coaching but weren't getting a great buy-in, and we wanted faster results with a more intentional focus.

We knew we had a sales problem. We had a limiting belief on how much we were worth because we were comparing ourselves to all other gyms out there. So we struggled with objection handling as well as making a compelling offer that would allow us to give the value needed.

AFTER PT LEGENDS & HIGH-TICKET:

As an owner, I personally have loved that my team is getting 3 hours of sales training, objections handling, and sale pitch practice.

Our nutrition program has become so much more valuable, streamlined, and it's really morphed into a full accountability (nutrition, sleep, mindset, lifestyle) type of program because the margins allow us to work on building out more. This has helped with retention having more layers to it.

I've been able to take two coaches who were working about 10 hours a week to both being around 32 hours a week just because of the PT legends program.

It gave us a true differentiator that we didn't have before compared to other boutique style gyms.

AMAZING HIGHLIGHTS:

We created an additional $54k in revenue from Transformation programs in the first 4 months.

Sold ten $1500 programs for our transformation challenges in ONE day (previously, we only charged $200 for that).

We've helped two. clients officially be able to stop insulin and they are no longer considered Type 2 diabetic.

CHAPTER 3
HOW TO MULTIPLY YOUR PRICE

"Coke, it costs money. Planes, they cost money. This yacht, this perm, my kid's braces, it all costs money!"
— Reese Feldman, Starsky & Hutch

There is a good chance you already have add-ons to increase your average client spend per month.

You may have some type of nutrition add-on, at $99-$199 per month. You may potentially have supplements or other ancillary products.

The problems you get with low-priced add-ons are the same problems as large group. The price isn't high enough for someone to be invested, and margins are incredibly low if you aren't the one performing the services. You have to do a lot of work for a low return. The juice isn't worth the squeeze, as they say.

And there is a problem with anything that is a low price point: your clients won't value it very much. $129/month for nutrition coaching just isn't a big investment. They'll probably lose interest and motivation after a few weeks. Retention will be a struggle. And you'll probably volunteer to check in with them multiple times per week to add value. Good luck scaling that and not burning the hell out!

You may have also had some price increases to your monthly membership rates. That definitely helps, but marginal price increases will only get you marginal results. We are not just looking to increase your prices by adding small percentages—we are going to MULTIPLY your prices for instant, massive additions to your bottom line.

You may already have some sort of "High-Ticket" offer. If you offer personal training, or in some cases small group or semi-private training, that's high-ticket. Common rates are $60-80/hr for one-on-one. Two times per week, rounding down to 8 sessions per month, is $480 to $640. Three times per week, 13 sessions per month comes to $780 to $1,040. That's getting up there, but it's not without its limitations.

Personal training, my bread and butter for years, also has its downsides. Almost everyone wants prime time hours, so you you'll have to continue to hire more staff to overcome that bottleneck. But that's not so easy, because it's really hard to fill their off-peak hours, and you can easily under-employ them.

While you can increase revenue quickly with personal training, renewals are very reliant on the quality of the trainer whom you hire. And if they can't make a livable wage, they'll eventually leave you. If you have PT clients now, you know exactly what happens if you lose the trainer: the relationship, and the business, goes away. If you lose a key staff member, it's common to see $6,000 in monthly revenue disappear.

Let's get to the good news, though. If you already sell personal training, you're already technically selling a high-ticket item. We just have to take it to the next level. If you haven't sold it before, that's okay. You'll just have to work harder to overcome your own false beliefs about what people are willing to pay and what you and your services are truly worth.

The average CrossFit gym that implements our Price Multiplier Method will increase its large group rates by 6-11x with its Transformation Program, and double its personal training rates for an Accelerator Program. It gets *really* sexy with the Executive Program, which most sell for $6,000 to $8,000 for a 9-week program (some are even virtual programs, not in-house)!

There are five main components to the Price Multiplier Method. Over the next several chapters we'll walk you through each of them.

THE PRICE MULTIPLIER METHOD

The Transformational Offer: You'll need to learn how to create additional, bolt-on High-Ticket services and set your prices anywhere from $2,000 to $8,000.

The Doctor's Office: You'll learn how to stop playing defense and start playing offense with your leads and prospects. If you're going to sell High-Ticket offers, you're going to need to establish yourself as an expert and posture with authority.

The Sales Resurrection System: This is the big sexy. I'm going to walk you **through** our killer sales system that allows us to close High-Ticket offers at 70-80%—without sacrificing your normal options (group, semi, private, etc).

The Turn-Key Coaching System: Of course, you can't just sell something you don't know how to deliver. We'll teach you the nuts and bolts on how to fulfill your Transformation Program and deliver unprecedented results for your clients.

The Flawless Renewal System: One of the criticisms business mentors claim about our High-Ticket program is that, at a price point that high, renewals are unknown and could be potentially poor. This is 100% false. We'll show you the system we created that allows many CrossFit owners to achieve retention rates far beyond what they were seeing with their low-priced group memberships.

Ready to dig into the Price Multiplier System? Let's go!

MATTHEW CHENARD

Gym:

GREATER PURPOSE HEALTH & FITNESS

LOCATION: Camrose, Alberta Canada

IN BUSINESS FOR: 10 years

BEFORE PT LEGENDS & HIGH-TICKET:

We had trouble believing that someone would buy a higher priced program. We had little confidence and knowledge of being able to put a high-value service together.

AFTER PT LEGENDS & HIGH-TICKET:

PT Legends literally helped us get our gym through the pandemic. Our cashflow would have dried up if not for the program. I can see a way of creating a better environment for my coaches to succeed and be professionals in the industry.

Our business would have closed if it weren't for PT Legends.

AMAZING HIGHLIGHTS:

Sold $32k of new sales in 2.5 weeks.

Built a new $100k revenue stream in under 9 months.

CHAPTER 4

CREATING A HIGH-TICKET TRANSFORMATIONAL OFFER

Michael Bolton: You think the pet rock was a really great idea?

Tom Smykowski: Sure it was. The guy made a million dollars. You know, I had an idea like that once. A long time ago.

Peter Gibbons: Really, what was it, Tom?

Tom Smykowski: Well, all right. It was a "Jump to Conclusions" mat. You see, it would be this mat that you would put on the floor, and it would have different conclusions written on it that you could jump to.

— Office Space

As a CrossFit gym, your main offer, or what you sell, is amazing workouts. You sell mainly group memberships, right?

And many of you also offer nutrition coaching, small group or semi-private, and possibly some one-on-one personal training.

And that seems like a good idea—because when leads contact you, whether over the phone or from your website form, they typically just want to know the price and what times your classes are.

So it seems like you're giving them what they want, right? Well, that's exactly the problem.

You are jumping to conclusions. What your potential leads think they want and need isn't in fact what they actually want and need.

In their heads, they're thinking something like, "I feel crappy about myself. I'm fat and out of shape. I need to start working out."

And then, they call your gym and ask what your prices are.

But that's not what they really want and what they really need. Deep down they know that.

They think they need to start working out because that is the only way they know to start solving their problem. Some may even think they also need to follow a diet.

They'll say, "I know what I need to do, I just need to do it."

But as you know, the typical American knows exactly jack shit about what it takes to make a transformation and create the lifelong habits needed to keep results.

You do. So you can't leave it up to them to tell you what they need. You can't let them say, "I know what I need to do, I just need to do it." They've struggled for years upon years with this problem.

If you start peeling back the layers of the onion, you'll find out much more. They'll come to you and say they really need to start working out. But what if you explore further? Why do they want to start working out? Because they realize they're getting out of shape or letting themselves go, and need to lose weight and get healthy.

You're getting closer, but keep digging. Why do they need to lose weight and get healthy? Because they are insecure about how they look and feel, are tired, and it's affecting how they show up in life as a spouse, a parent, at work, as a friend.

The real reason they are contacting your gym is because they are **unhappy with themselves**. And unless they make serious changes with their mindset, daily habits, exercise, and nutrition, they are unlikely to see any lasting change.

In essence, it's not only about the external change of weight loss, smaller clothing sizes, more energy, getting stronger, or having more endurance. Those are amazing things, but what clients really want is to change internally. They want to make an identity change.

That's what we call the **bleeding neck issue**. If you can find their bleeding neck issue, and get them to understand what it's costing them if they don't resolve it, their price resistance will disappear and you can sell your current services thousands of dollars.

They don't just want to get from point A to point B— they want to *become* the person they really want to be. Someone with confidence. Someone who works out three times a week and eats healthy as a lifestyle. Someone who starts the day with purpose and drive and acts on the right habits, because they know that's what it takes to live their best life.

So *that's* your offer. That's what you are selling. Your offer is to solve the **bleeding neck issue**—to overcome what is holding them back from living their best life. You are offering an identity change, not just results.

THE WORKOUTS AREN'T ENOUGH

If you are in the current habit of trying to add value by talking about how much better your workouts are than other competitors, you might not like this fact.

But it's true nonetheless. You and I know the clients who have come in 3-5 times per week religiously for months and years, and have never made any progress when it comes to weight loss or body confidence.

If you really look at the clients who actually make a true transformation—who will tell other people that coming to your gym, and working with you or your coaches, has given them a second lease on life—they are the ones who have made the necessary changes outside of your four walls. They've modified their nutrition and habits, and have had an internal motivation to drive them.

Unfortunately, only 5-10% of your clients will see true transformations, no matter how hard you try and no matter how good your workouts are.

While the workouts are a necessary component, they are massively overrated. As a CrossFit gym owner, you probably believe that your functional workouts are superior to many other kinds of workouts. And you're probably right, and wrong, at the same time.

You see, it's not about the workouts. At least 90% of your clients aren't here for the workouts. So, stop making that your "thing." Stop telling them that your workouts are better. They don't care!

The only want their bleeding neck issue solved. And there are 168 hours in a week. Will working out for 3 hours per week change their lives? Of course not. You have clients who have worked out 3 times per week for years and have hardly made any changes.

It's the other 165 hours in the week, outside of your four walls, that are the most important. That's what gets the amazing results, and that's what your Transformation Offer solves.

CREATING YOUR HIGH-TICKET OFFER

So you're thinking—great, it makes perfect sense. But how do I even do that?

The answer is easier than you might think.

I have all my CrossFit gym owner clients provide a 3-offer approach for their bolt-on Transformation Programs.

Remember: you DO NOT have to change your business model. Transformational Programs won't replace everything you do now. You don't have to stop offering your large group classes, small group or semi-private, and one-on-one personal training.

At a high level, your different Transformational offers are exactly the same exercise options you already have—you are just adding nutrition, accountability, motivation, and mindset onto these options in the form of a mentorship.

Many of you have Group + Nutrition, or Personal Training + Nutrition, and the price for these are the logical sums of what each one is individually. Your price sheets are usually complicated tables involving all the different combinations of options, frequency, and add-ons.

DO NOT do this. The buying decision is a very emotional one. Remember, people don't care *how* you get them from point A to point B—they just want to get there.

Your consults are buying based on their emotional needs. If you perform your consults correctly, they'll be in a heightened emotional state. The last thing you want to do is show them nine options in different columns, followed by ten rows of checks indicating what you get versus what you don't for each of the options.

If you do that, you'll shift them into an analytical state. They'll start weighing price versus value, what they need versus what they can do on their own, and start to veer away from what is really important, the WHY, not the how.

In addition, too many options lead people to need to "think about it."

Take the Jam Experiment from 2000, for example. Psychologists Sheena Iyengar from Columbia University and Mark Lepper from Stanford set up two tables at a food market, one with 6 different types of jams and one with 24 different types of jams.

While the table with 24 jams generated more visitors and more interest, they sold about 10 times fewer jars of jam.

Choice can paralyze the customer.

Keep. It. Simple.

Here's what a sample price sheet looks like for a CrossFit gym:

EXECUTIVE TRANSFORMATION

$7,000

ACCELERATOR PROGRAM

$4,000

TRANSFORMATION PROGRAM

$3,000

Pretty simple, right?

Now don't worry, you can still have all your original options on separate pages as a backup. You'll still sell those options under the right circumstances. But for Transformations, this is all you need.

If you start listing everything you get in each option, people will stop listening to you and start analyzing. That's the last thing you want them to be doing in the buying decision.

WHAT'S IN A TRANSFORMATIONAL OFFER

For all three options, what we fulfill on the back end is virtually the same.

Included are 3x/week workouts, 1 one-on-one onboarding session, and a weekly mentoring check-in (typically 20-30 minutes).

That's it. That's all you need to do to coach and educate someone to see massive changes. The only thing that varies between the options is the delivery of the workout (the Executive Transformation option has another small change we'll get into in a bit).

If you look at the bottom option, Transformation Program, I have CrossFit gyms deliver their workouts in their large group format.

For the Accelerator option, I have CrossFit gyms deliver their workouts in either a semi-private or a one-on-one format. Whatever you are doing now is generally the best way for you to start.

There is also another format I created, one that has all the pros of one-on-one and semi-private, but none of the cons each inherently possesses. They each have their strengths and weaknesses, but overlapping personal training will solve massive long-term problems with both—perceived value, set time constraints, capacity limitations of 1:1—and therefore hiring, employee pay caps, and so on.

This new format has completely changed my gyms, to the point where, as personal training studios, we no longer even offer one-on-one. If you are curious to learn more about this, you can find episodes on The PT Legends podcast (www.ptlegends.com/podcast) where I talk about this format.

A word of caution though: DO NOT get hung up learning about this and getting in a rush to apply it into your business. Get your High-Ticket Transformation offer going now. Then, look into improving your profit, margins, capacity, and employee compensation with this model.

The reason I am not expanding on this topic in this book is because this is not your limitation right now. Taking the next one to two months learning and implementing a change like this at this moment will be a distraction from the hard, important work of creating and selling a high-ticket offer in your business. First things first!

THE MENTORSHIP

Coaching and mentoring clients to success sounds great; we all want to bring out our inner Tony Robbins and help people change. But, as you know, it's HARD.

Most people just don't want to put in the work and make the hard changes outside of the gym. The ones who do are typically very motivated internally. Even though they credit us as the reason they've changed, we all know that they are one of the few who followed our instructions and put in the work with nutrition and everything else. One of the *very* few.

And remember, we want true, lasting change. Not just the external results (weight loss, increased energy and strength) that we'll call ACHIEVEMENT in the Iceberg of Success graphic on the following page, but internal results (identity change) that we'll call TRANSFORMATION.

Everyone is familiar with the iceberg metaphor. Everything above the water is the success that you see, and everything below the water is the hard work that goes into it which no one witnesses.

Transformation

Achievement

Environment

Habits

Strength Training   Daily Movement   Nutrition   Routines

Mindset

When you look at this graphic, you can see how incredibly easy it is for a client to see why they've failed over, and over, and over again year after year. Or why they keep losing and gaining back the same ten to twenty pounds.

This graphic shows that the workouts, and making temporary dietary changes, is just a small part of what it takes to create lasting change—a lasting TRANSFORMATION.

So let's take a quick look into the different components.

MINDSET

It all starts with mindset. Clients must WANT and DESIRE to change, not just sign up for a group membership and hope shit works out.

Our Sales Resurrection System starts the process. If you don't set things up correctly, they'll never truly buy in. By establishing your business as The Doctor's Office and performing the Discovery Call, in The Perfect Consult you will help them establish WHY they NEED to make this change, and what it will cost them if they don't take action now.

Connecting with WHY they need to make this change is so important. If you don't do this properly, your clients will never be receptive to the changes you need them to make.

HABITS

If your client is at starting point A, and they want to get to destination point B, all it comes down to is identifying and taking the necessary actions every day and week that will get them there.

All you need to do is build their perfect day and week which will lead them to the results they desire.

Typically, you'll have workouts, daily movement, a nutrition strategy, and routines or structure as a part of their plan. Week after week, you'll help them build these actions into their daily lives so they become new, healthy habits which will service them for a lifetime.

ENVIRONMENT

Not many people succeed alone. When you are surrounded by people who support you, your chances go up dramatically.

When clients join your gym, they'll be integrated with supportive people who are on a similar path. In addition, they'll also have a mentor who will walk with them through this journey every step of the way.

WHAT ABOUT ONLINE OR VIRTUAL HIGH-TICKET OFFERS?

Remember, workouts are a necessary component to change, but they are definitely not the most important part.

Whether the workouts are delivered in one-on-one personal training, semi-private, small group, or large group—does it really matter?

Not really. If your clients are taking all the right actions outside of your four walls, they'll get amazing results regardless of the delivery of the workouts.

That's why we use the EXACT same process for all our online training. Instead of having them come in for the workouts, we build and send them the workouts to do on their own, whether they work out at home, an apartment gym, or have a membership to a full-access gym.

Whether you deliver the workouts in the form of a PDF, written with links to the exercises, or through TrueCoach, Trainerize, or any other software is up to you.

The workouts are simply overrated. The value is in the mentoring. Just follow the same process with the onboarding call and the weekly mentoring calls.

So how much should you charge for online-only, virtual programs? Well, you already know from Chapter 2 that charging anywhere from ninety-nine to a few hundred bucks isn't going to cut it.

Maybe you have the intention of taking on virtual clients only when they come your way via referrals from existing clients. But maybe you also do want to grow and scale an online training business. In order to do so, you're going to need money to pay to advertise, help with creating social media content with graphics and video, and eventually hire staff to help you with outreach, appointment booking, sales, advertising, accountability and mentoring check-ins, and everything else.

It is only possible for you to do this, and run your physical location, if you charge enough to afford these services.

Our Legends sell their 9-week virtual programs anywhere from $3,000 to $8,000.

Yep. That much. With no in-person workouts included.

Taryn, a completely badass Legend, sold her Executive Transformation for $8,000 to a particularly qualified lead. He loved it so much that he brought his wife in to do the virtual Accelerator Program. Then, they committed to doing this for an entire year.

But it gets even better. They PAID IN FULL.

Taryn just received a payment of $90,000—and it only costs her two Zoom calls per week.

How crazy is that? That's from the result of one initial lead.

How would making an extra $90,000 this year change your life?

FEATURED LEGEND

JAY COHEN

Gym:

LOCOMOTION FITNESS

LOCATION: Charleston, SC

IN BUSINESS FOR: 7 years

BEFORE PT LEGENDS & HIGH-TICKET:

I didn't know how to sell or add on high-ticket programs. I wasn't sure how to build the packages. I had no clue how to build the assets needed to deliver.

This was something I always wanted to do but didn't know how to do it.

AFTER PT LEGENDS & HIGH-TICKET:

It has given me the confidence to create new businesses and revenue streams after feeling stuck for a long time. I now know that High-Ticket coaching is where my heart lies—and this is where I can best use my talents.

AMAZING HIGHLIGHTS:

$40k in revenue in 60 days post launch.

Over 60% margin on that revenue.

CHAPTER 5

RUN YOUR GYM LIKE A DOCTOR'S OFFICE

*"You and your mother are a bunch of hillbillies.
This is a house of learned doctors."*
— Dale Doback, Step Brothers

Ring ring.

"This is Northwest CrossFit, Scott speaking, how can I help you?"

"I just wanted to ask, what are the prices for your classes?"

TIME OUT!
(ZACK MORRIS SAVED BY THE BELL STYLE)

Have you been in this situation before? Yes, you have. Where do you go from here? You're at a massive disadvantage from the start. You're either forced to dodge the question, or answer it quickly and immediately go on to try and build value in what you do and how you're different in hopes that you can book the caller in for a consultation.

The good news is that this is what every single gym and fitness studio will do. You have a massive opportunity to do something different and set yourself apart.

When people call into one of my gyms, we never talk to them on the phone then and there, and we typically have the same policy for walk-ins. All they're going to do is ask your price—and when they do that, they are completely in control.

If you're letting your customers control the sales process from the start, you're fighting a losing battle. You're immediately on the defense when you're allowing them to interview you to see if you check their boxes. What times are classes? Do you have showers there? How many people are in your classes? How experienced are your coaches and trainers? And so on and so on.

But typically, they'll just want to know the price. They have no idea what separates a good gym from a bad gym. They have no idea what their real problem is or what they actually need to fix it.

But here you are, playing defense.

This is *horrible* for two reasons.

1. It erodes your authority as an expert

2. People have no idea what they actually need

Johnny Lawrence, from *Cobra Kai*, says "The best defense is more offense." I'm going to have to agree with Johnny here.

FLIP THE SCRIPT & PLAY OFFENSE

Let's say you have a neck injury, and after spending five minutes on WebMD you decide you need surgery. So, you call or stop by the doctor's office, demand to speak to the surgeon, tell him or her what you think is wrong, self-prescribe the surgery you need, and ask what the prices are and if you can come in tomorrow morning before work.

Could you actually get away with that? Hell no! You have to follow their system. You have to call, give them your information, make an appointment, fill out forms prior to your visit, and come in to their business when the doctor is available to see you.

He or she then listens to what you have to say, but asks more questions and runs tests to find out what's really going on. How long have you been feeling this way? Was it a gradual increase in pain or was it a result of an impact? Does it hurt when you move it up and down? Side to side or rotationally? Has this ever happened in your past?

The doctor's job is to identify the source of your issue, diagnose the problem, and prescribe a solution. She is the expert on the subject, not you as the patient. You're following her office's entire process, then you get her prescription, and finally you get to the price.

People listen to doctors. They are at the very top of the authority scale in our society, for good or bad (I'm sure you've wanted to smack your head when a doctor advised one of your clients to stop working out for stupid reasons). They are professional and are rarely questioned.

Compare that to us as fitness professionals. How many times has a client interrupted you as you were coaching them on nutrition to "contribute" to the conversation and start telling *you* things about nutrition? The reason they do this is because we don't enjoy the same level of authority and expertise as doctors do.

But here's the thing—you *are* the expert.

Part of the reason people don't see you this way is because you aren't running your business like a professional office.

I can't just call up the office and speak to the doctor. He's busy and has more important things going on. And there's a good chance, if a doctor is just hanging out when I pop in at 10:00 a.m. and can talk to me for 15 – 60 minutes and answer all my questions, that I may doubt if he's the right fit.

YOU NEED TO RUN YOUR BUSINESS LIKE A DOCTOR'S OFFICE.

You need to establish authority as the expert in your community. You need to play offense rather than defense.

Here's how we do it: when someone calls in to the studio, we answer the phone. Of course, all they're going to do is ask the price. Generally, we'll say something like:

"Hey [name], I'm glad you called. I'm just heading into an appointment / Zoom coaching session / podcast / meeting. The way we start is by setting up a quick 7-minute phone call to learn what you're looking to do and to see if you'd be a good fit for one of our programs. I have 10:15 or 2:50 open for the call. Which works better for you?"

This will put *you* in control of the process and begin to position yourself as an authority. It will also allow you to interview them on the phone call— *they'll* answer *your* questions instead of the other way around. When you master this 7-minute call (more on this in the next chapter), they won't even get a chance to ask the price before coming in. You'll be shocked at how empowered you feel from this call. It completely changes the relationship.

What about web leads, you ask? We use the exact same process, regardless of whether they were organic website leads, or whether they came in as a result of an add or funnel.

The first text message that goes out to the lead will look like this:

Hi Tascha,

This is Scott from NorthWest CrossFit. I'm finishing my afternoon and just received your inquiry.

Before we invite potential clients into the studio for a consult, we do a quick discovery call to make sure you are a good fit for one of our programs. When are you available to chat this evening?

Have a great day!

Scott

The exact script may look different for your business depending on manual texting versus autoresponders, who in your company handles inbound leads, manual appointment booking versus auto-booking, etc.—but you get the idea.

Now you'll be in a position to play offense rather than defense. You'll be the one in control, asking the questions, and determining if the prospect is a good fit for your business (more on that in Part I of The Sales Resurrection System).

When you put these fundamentals into practice, you'll *feel* the difference. You will feel empowered; you will feel the confidence, belief, certainty, and conviction you need to be the expert in your field.

WHAT IF SOMEONE DOESN'T RESPECT YOUR PROCESS?

As a fellow gym owner, I know that you've experienced your share of crazies over time. I'm not sure what brings so many people who are nuts into our industry, but it is what it is.

Stay true to your process. Anyone who doesn't respect your process will never respect you or your business, and will ultimately be someone you don't want to work with.

I had a prospect I was communicating with over Facebook Messenger. After she expressed interest in coming in, I let her know that the first step was to book a call to make sure she was a good candidate.

She responded saying that she didn't like phone calls, and just wanted to come in.

Most affiliate owners (and certainly me in the past!), not being wildly profitable and having a bit of a scarcity mindset, would just book a consultation with this prospect.

After all, the customer is always right… Right?

I stuck to my guns, and explained that the reason we set up a call before we invite people in is because we have limited openings, and first we want to make sure she is a good fit to protect her time as well as ours.

Well, of course she didn't like that, and messaged back saying she would be going elsewhere.

Curiosity got the better of me, so I took a dive into her online profile. Suffice it to say, there was ample evidence to show that I dodged a bullet. We would not have meshed well and her aggressive, controversial opinions would have clashed with our company culture.

Can you imagine having to deal with, in your gym, having to deal with someone whose vibe completely pisses you off?

Life is too short to put up with people like this. Stick to the process. Stick to your guns. Run your business like a Doctor's Office.

LAUREN BLACK

Gym:

ROCKTOWN CROSSFIT

LOCATION: Harrisonburg, VA

IN BUSINESS FOR: 9 years

BEFORE PT LEGENDS & HIGH-TICKET:

Lack of a clear system that provided a premium service, lack of confidence in selling high-ticket items, providing "the total package" where everything was rolled into one (nutrition, mindset, workouts, ect)…we had been selling and offering them as parts of the package.

AFTER PT LEGENDS & HIGH-TICKET:

The obvious: an increase in revenue. My clients are getting better results on this program because they are paying for it and more invested, but it's looking at EVERYTHING so nothing can fall through the cracks. It's given me confidence to sell and charge what I'm worth. :)

AMAZING HIGHLIGHTS:

I sold more in these packages in the month of December (my first full month with PT Legends) than the rest of my gym's services combined.

I sold 16K in 31 days which led to a PR month in revenue.

HIGH TICKET FOR AFFILIATE GYMS

CHAPTER 6
THE SALES RESURRECTION SYSTEM PART I:
THE 7-MINUTE MICROWAVE

"We're doing the interview now, not you."
— *Brennan Huff, Step Brothers*

You're in one of two camps when it comes to sales. You know you're pretty damn good at it, or you know that you definitely could use some help.

I've been "pretty damn good" at sales for quite some time. When I got into personal training management at Life Time Fitness, a good part of my job was selling for other trainers (definitely a bit more challenging than selling for yourself).

Selling group training, personal training sessions at $99, and any ancillary product or service you could think of was good practice for when I set out on my own. I racked up hundreds of hours of experience very quickly.

As a gym owner, I was great at selling personal training— our 2x, 3x, or 4x per week at $600, $840, or $1040 monthly.

And when I wasn't able to get those, I'd sell our semi-private training at standard market rates, anywhere from $280 to $480.

Not bad. But—that's a far cry from selling a 9-Week (3x/wk semi-private) Executive Transformation for $6,000. Or even an Accelerator Transformation for $3,000, which comes out to $111/session for semi-private training.

And our CrossFit gym owners often sell their GROUP Transformations at $2,000 (for a 9 to 12-week program).

If you're selling 3x/wk group CrossFit, plus 1 one-on-one Onboarding Session, and a quick 15-20 minute mentoring call per week, for $2,000...

You're going to need to up your sales game—even if you are already "pretty damn good."

You need new techniques, you need to have belief and certainty in what you are doing, and most importantly, you need to get in reps.

Dave, the Kool-Aid Man, and I created The Sales Resurrection System to bring your sales back from the dead.

You don't need to be fighting and scrambling and convincing someone to pay you $150/month.

You need to become a Sales Jedi and crush $3k deals.

There are just three simple steps:

The 7-Minute Microwave (The Discovery Call)

The Perfect Consultation

The Invincible Pitch

I'll walk you through each of these over the next three chapters.

THE 7-MINUTE MICROWAVE (THE DISCOVERY CALL)

Remember in Chapter 5 when we mentioned that you need to run your business like a Doctor's Office?

That is important so you're playing offense, not defense. You need to control the sales process. Your prospects will feel much more at ease when they know you are controlling the process—that you have a proven method which will take care of all their problems.

The 7-Minute Microwave (typically I'll refer to it as a Discovery Call) is the first step in the sales process. It's just a quick, 7-minute phone call you have with each prospect before you agree to have them come in for a no-sweat intro, goal planning session, or whatever you call your consultation.

I know you may be thinking that this sounds like extra work, an extra step to have to do. You'd rather just book them (or auto-book them if you do that with software) straight in for the consultation.

But you know as well as I do that, in general, people want to get to know each other first before just hopping into bed together.

It's no different here. Remember—your prospect contacted you because they think that working out will solve their problems. They don't even have a clue to what their real problem is yet. You have to open them up to that, and to do this you need to establish authority, build trust, and show them the bigger picture.

You aren't going to achieve this by merely answering their questions about pricing or class times.

So, before you make your call first, put on your lab coat and become the Doctor. Get in your own head, and hype yourself up over this. I know it sounds dumb, but really visualize yourself as the top expert in your field. Imagine you are running the most sought-after surgical practice in the world, and you get to pick who you choose to have for your clients.

Then dial the number.

The idea here is to move this call along quickly and control the process. If you do this correctly, 99% of the time they won't get a chance to ask about pricing. You'll keep it nice and tight, your prospect will be highly impressed, and you'll make your Perfect Consultation incredibly easy.

You can build small-talk rapport on the weather, or what neighborhood they live in, or some other chitchat, but keep it really tight (30-60 seconds max).

Then, get the call on track by letting them know you have another call or appointment in ten minutes, so you'll have to stick to time. The goal here is to act busy, but polite (don't be a dick).

Then just get right to it. Tell them the purpose of the call.

"I'm going to ask you a few questions to determine if you would be a good fit for one of my programs. If you are, we'll take the next step and I'll invite you to come into the gym, and together we'll sit down and start building out what a program would look like for you. Sound good?"

Can you see how in control of this process you are? How certain you are of your proven process? How unexpected, yet comforting this is for the person with a bleeding neck issue?

Remember, you're in control and asking the questions, so keep the momentum going.

Keep in mind that it's not always what you say, it's how you say it. Slow down, emphasize the words, bring some passion and feeling into your message.

"So tell me, why are we on the call today? What are you struggling the most with right now in terms of your health and fitness? Is it workouts, your nutrition, accountability, motivation, or is it a little bit of everything?"

Do you see what I just did here? I teed the ball up for them to say that it's all a bit of a mess—they haven't been working out, their eating habits are way off, and they're not living their best lives.

More often than not, this will open the gates for your prospects to start telling you about their pain and giving you some great insight into their bleeding neck issue.

Next, you'll want to ask another question to establish a gap between where they are now, and where they would like to be. It's important to help them realize there is a bigger gap than they had originally thought. You'll understand why when we dive into the Perfect Consultation.

Finally, you'll ask them if solving this problem is a "now" thing or a "later" thing. You're looking for them to say it's a now thing and qualify them.

If you determine they're a good fit for you as a client, the next step is to let them know that. Let them know that the goal of the call was to see if we could help you, and the good news is that they are a great fit for what you do.

Let them know that the next step is to schedule your in-person meeting to do a deep dive into building out what a program would look like for them.

But before you get off the phone, you're going to need to give them some homework. DO NOT skip this part. This will make your Perfect Consultation far easier when you execute this ask at a high level.

"To inspire starts with the clarity of WHY."
—Simon Sinek

The homework you're going to assign is for them to send you their 3-5 reasons WHY they want to make this change. The *real* reasons why they want to change, not just the surface-level answers, like they want to look better in a bikini or with their shirt off. Have them send their answers to you as a prerequisite (remember, keep a strong Doctor Frame) before they come in for the Perfect Consultation.

When you successfully pitch them this homework, you'll get text messages like these:

Well it's a little stream of consciousness and chaotic but I just wrote what I thought and didn't edit it lol.

1.   Confidence. I want my confidence back. I am embarrassed to even leave the house. I feel ashamed that I have let myself get to be this size. I think my family is embarrassed to be seen with me. I used to be one of the most confident people and I miss that. I embarrassed to be seen naked. I wear sweatpants and sweatshirts even when it's hot just to hide my body. I skip out on parties and get togethers just because I am ashamed of how I look now.

2.   My children. I want to show my children that I am healthy and that I take pride in my health, not just theirs. I want to show them that it's important to take care of yourself too and not just of everyone around you. I want to be a good example to them and I don't think I'm being one right now in this aspect.

3.   Energy. I am constantly drained. Of all the things I can count

  iMessage

on in life, the most consistent one is that I am perpetually exhausted. I believe my mental state has something to do with this as well and I think it's all stemmed from my overall health and constant obsession over how I look and feel right now.

4. My mind. I feel like all I think about all day every day is how awful I feel. How my body feels heavy and gross. How tired I am. How embarrassed I am. I want to feel good about myself to the point where I'm not so fixated on it anymore. Where my mind can feel free of this constant burden. I feel as though my thoughts are out of my control and I want to take that control back.

5. The love of my life. I am too embarrassed to really let myself go when being intimate anymore. I am completely in my head and self conscious the whole time. The past year has been slowly getting worse and worse and I know it's affecting us. I also want him to respect me more like he used to but I think the way I talk about myself and look like

  iMessage

way I talk about myself and look like
I don't care about myself makes it
hard for anyone to respect me.
Subconsciously or not. I want him to
know that I care about myself and
that I am important too.

6. Because I deserve this. I am
a good person. I am an excellent
mother and partner. I bust my ass
for everyone around me everyday
and I deserve to bust my ass for
myself too. I deserve to feel good
about how I look and I deserve to
feel healthy and energetic.

Mon, May 24, 11:33 AM

I love this!!! Your honesty is
incredibly brave, and 100%

iMessage

Can you see how getting answers like this before your consultation completely changes the game?

You know exactly where to go in the consultation; it's your battle plan. This lays out the bleeding neck issue.

And what does this do for your confidence when selling a high-ticket program? When you're looking at the problems this prospect is facing, ask yourself: Is it worth $3,000 to solve those problems?

Hell, yeah it is! It's worth way more!

It takes a while to make this 7-Minute Microwave your own. It takes practice to not let this turn into a 15 to 20-minute call or longer.

But the quicker, tighter, and more in control of this call you are, the better your results will be. Remember, you're a busy-ass Doctor. You're not an asshole—you're just pressed for time and can't wait to meet them in person.

If you take command and control the call, it is very rare that the prospect will get a chance to ask about price. If you are uncertain, and have many pauses, they'll typically take control and ask questions instead of the other way around.

It takes practice. It takes reps. It takes refinement. Master this call and you'll see how much easier your consultations will get.

When Dave Bess and I first started implementing the Discovery Call into our first location in Glendale, Arizona—even before we were any good at this process, before we mastered the Perfect Consultation, or even sold our High-Ticket programs for more than $2,000—Dave, the Kool-Aid Man himself, sold just over $40,000 in new business in the first four weeks of adding the Discovery Call.

We didn't change any marketing. We didn't change any websites, calls to action, or any auto-responders. We solely changed what we did with the leads when they came in by adding a Discovery Call, performing the Perfect Consultation, and selling a High-Ticket Transformational Offer.

Don't worry about changing all your marketing and automations—you don't need to do that right now (or even at all!).

Just take action!

Refinements and mastery will come with time.

SARA CARTER

Gym:

PORTSIDE FITNESS

LOCATION: Gulfport, MS

IN BUSINESS FOR: 9 years

BEFORE PT LEGENDS & HIGH-TICKET:

Before joining PT Legends, I was stuck working more in my gym then really on the gym. I sold the typical group memberships as well as hybrid memberships which included nutrition. We were also doing a decent amount of Personal Training. I was at a cross roads about what I really wanted to do. I was ready to get out of my comfort zone and really change people's lives. I knew I could see high-ticket transformations but also wasn't sure in the deep south that it was possible. Boy, was I wrong!

AFTER PT LEGENDS & HIGH-TICKET:

The biggest impact has been on our transformation clients. It is absolutely incredible the things that are happening. We even had a client reach out to someone after 16 years of not speaking to them. What an impact!!!

I have more freedom with my time as I am able to hand off all the fulfillment to my coaches, and I give them an opportunity to really make some good money doing what they love. I am able to pay myself plenty and put money away and in investments. I was stuck in the same place for years. It is awesome to feel like things are paying off. I have changed as a leader, as a person, as a mentor to my coaches. I have become more passionate about Portside all over again.

AMAZING HIGHLIGHTS:

I had never hit about $25k in revenue in my 9 years. 2 months in I hit $37k and have had multiple $30k months.

I have had more people tell me that this has changed their life and I am mostly proud of that over the revenue! I have found my niche with menopausal women and I am so excited to continue to help them along their journey.

CHAPTER 7

THE SALES RESURRECTION SYSTEM PART II: THE PERFECT CONSULTATION

"I'm pretty sure there's a lot more to life than being really, really,
ridiculously good looking. And I plan on finding out what that is."
— Derek Zoolander, *Zoolander*

Chances are, you're already doing some of the right things in your consultations. But there is *always* room to improve—especially when you're selling $2,000 to $8,000 short-term programs.

Selling $150-$400 monthly memberships is no big deal—but when selling high-ticket you're going to have to get comfortable being uncomfortable and level up.

I'm always reminded of the famous Alec Baldwin scene in the sales drama *Glengarry Glen Ross*, when he's giving a speech to three salesmen:

"You know what it takes to sell real estate?"

[he pulls out two spheres on a string and holds them over his crotch, pausing for a moment]

"It takes brass balls to sell real estate."

That may be a tad dramatic, but the point I'm trying to make here is that for many CrossFit gym owners, selling a High-Ticket offer is going to require some [brass balls] confidence.

If you already sell a fair amount of personal training along with your group memberships, congratulations—you're already selling high-ticket!

If you really only sold low-priced memberships, you're going to experience more fear asking for the sale… at first.

You can, will, and must overcome this fear. It's normal, it's natural, and hell—even I had this fear when I began selling this—and I had previously sold over a million dollars of personal training.

It's going to take reps to get comfortable asking for thousands of dollars. I've taught many, many gym owners and their staff how to sell these programs. It's scary at first, no doubt about it. But once you make your first sale, the proof is right before your eyes. And once you take a couple clients through the fulfillment side of it, it all makes perfect sense. These people will get better results than anyone else you've tried to help in the past—and then you'll KNOW you're worth the price tag.

You'll have your "ah-ha" moment, and you'll understand how necessary this program is, why it *has* to cost this much, and you'll know your true worth.

Some gym owners are going to have this "ah-ha" moment in their first week, and for others it takes two months, but nothing is more powerful than when the switch flips and you're a different person for life. You, and your business, change forever.

When you know you can produce thousands of dollars out of thin air, and do so regularly, the fear of lead flow suddenly doesn't hold as much power over you. When you know that in two sales you can bring in $4,000 to $12,000 in new business revenue (quite often more new business than you've ever brought in on your best month in history), things change.

You can breathe easier. I know I have. While I've been doing well with my six gyms for quite some time, I've always carried that fear with me. I've always had that feeling that I was one bad break away from having to go back in to a gym and work full time. When we bolted on a High-Ticket offer and followed the Price Multiplier Method in this book, everything changed for me. I know that even when the "perfect storm" of negative events hits, it's not really a big deal. Losing key employees, pandemic shutdowns, an algorithm change that slashes my leads... I can recover from anything extremely quickly when I can make the equivalent selling multiple dozens of memberships in a single consultation.

So, let's get to learning how to deliver a Perfect Consultation. You're armed with your High-Ticket Transformational Offer, you've taken control and established your Doctor's Office with the prospect, you had a killer 7-Minute Discovery Call, and now you've received your prospect's "whys" via text before the big show, the Perfect Consultation.

Your job in Perfect Consultation is to act like the Doctor. You need to get to the root cause of their pain: the bleeding neck issue. You need to reveal to them how much it's costing them by not solving the real issue. You will show them that simply working out and/or following a diet is just a band-aid. And finally, you'll show them that your High-Ticket offer is the only solution that will help them solve their bleeding neck issue.

Ready to dive in? Let's go through the steps:

STEP 1: PUT YOUR SCRUBS ON

Before the consultation, review your client's "whys." Sometimes you'll get very juicy whys and the bleeding neck issue is easy to find (see an example on page 92). Other times, the answers will be more surface-level and you'll have to do more digging in the consultation. Either way, review these whys and search for the bleeding neck, or where that bleeding neck could be hidden.

After quickly reviewing these, develop your game plan on what questions and follow-up questions you'll ask in the consultation that will open them up to talk about the bleeding neck and understand how critical it is for them to take action.

Next, put your scrubs on (metaphorically speaking). You need to get your mindset right. YOU are the Doctor. They have a serious condition, and it's your duty and responsibility to ask the difficult questions and prescribe the best solution for them. What you do is important and impactful, and they need you. Set aside your fears and scarcity mindset. This person needs you.

STEP 2: RAPPORT AND PRE-OBJECTIONS

We all know what rapport is and how important it can be. For many of us, it comes naturally to break the ice and make our prospect feel comfortable. For those who struggle with making small talk, it's easier than you think. Just make a comment about the traffic, the weather, a local event, or the time of season.

The whole point of this is to just get them to feel comfortable, to shake off the nervousness or apprehensions your prospect may have when coming in the doors. Sometimes we as fitness professionals forget how intimidating it is for someone to come in. Often, they've been working up the courage for months or even years. In their mind, they are thinking they're the only person who's going to be out of shape, and everyone will be staring at them because they can't keep up. In this case, I thank them for having the courage to make it in, and assure them they're just like everyone else—and that they have found the right place.

It should be easy for you to be comfortable with the person coming in because, after all, this is your second date. You already know a bit about each other, and feel comfortable, because of the Discovery Call.

We've all run into objections at closing. While there are many ways to approach objections handling, the best way to handle objections is to never even get them in the first place. If you ask some key questions up front, you're able to take away their easy excuses to tell you "no." Here are some common objections and questions you can ask to handle them upfront:

Location: Do you live close to the studio? How long have you lived here?

Trust: Have you ever trained before or is this something new?

Time: What does your current work schedule look like? Where do you work?

Motivation/Commitment: On a scale of 1-10, 10 being you're willing to do anything, how motivated are you to change?

Significant Other: Who's going to be the most excited for you when you reach your goal?

Will This Program Work? What have you tried in the past to lose weight? What specific workout programs and diets have you tried? Why didn't they work?

Note that their answers to these questions will supply you with plenty of ammunition to use against the objections if they do pop up at the end. I would love to get into advanced objection handling, but I could write an entire book on that subject (maybe someday I will).

However, like jiu-jitsu, there are many things you just can't fully learn in a book. Our PT Legends gym owners go through a weekly objection-handling Zoom call. You get sharp really quick when you're forced to tackle an objection live on a call with other gym owners! It's uncomfortable, but you level up fast.

That being said, the introductory questions above will help you minimize or squash the objections you may get later on.

Take note of their answers, because you may need to reference them if you do get an objection at the end.

STEP 3: THE HELL

We want to transition into the real reason that they're here. As humans, we are terrific liars to ourselves. We are professionals at downplaying our own problems, dismissing how bad they are, and living life as if they don't exist. Your job in this step is to get potential clients to realize that what they think is just a flesh wound is actually a much bigger problem. It's a bleeding neck issue, and they need to solve it NOW. Your job is to poke around and reveal this to them—how painful it really is—their "Hell."

Start by either asking again—"What's not working with your health and fitness? What are you struggling with?"—or by restating the answer they gave you in the Discovery Call and asking them to expand on it.

Next, we want to dig into the specifics. This may be uncomfortable to ask, but it's important we confront the facts as they are and put a number to them. If we don't do that, we allow the person to continue to lie to themselves. These are great questions to get to the specifics on the past and present:

"What is your current weight?/What weight are you comfortable at?/What is your goal weight?"

"How long have you been at your current weight?/What has been the trend of your weight the past three years?"

"What did you eat yesterday?/How many times have you lost ten pounds?"

Next, you're going to get to the meat of it all: the bleeding neck issue. You're going to dig into the real reason why they're here, and the whys they sent you in the text message. Some of your prospects will open up freely and let it pour out. For others, you'll have to tease it out.

What's important is to let this be a conversation, not an interview. Don't just pepper them with questions—let it flow naturally and ask natural follow-up questions to probe deeper. If you're getting only surface-level answers, sometimes you'll have to get uncomfortable and ask some difficult and personal questions. It takes practice to work up the nerve to ask the "brass balls" questions. You'll get better and better at this with reps.

If you're sitting down with Tony Robbins to work on overcoming your limitations and change your life, do you think he's going to let you get away with bullshit answers? Nope! So don't let your prospects get away with it either.

Here are a few questions you can ask to probe deeper:

"What is the weight really costing you?"

"How is your self confidence? How is your social confidence? Do you feel like you are missing out on life?"

"What do you see when you look in the mirror? How do you feel when you look in the mirror?"

"Do you have purpose to your day? When was the last time you were excited to get out of bed?"

"When was the last time you were happy?"

Remember, this is a conversation. Don't roll through this like a script. Sometimes your prospect will just spew out everything wrong in their lives, and sometimes you'll have to ease them into opening up.

Once you've talked about the bleeding neck, ask a couple questions to ratchet up the "Hell" that they're in:

"What is the worst part about being in your current situation?"

"What does your life look like if you don't take action?"

Next, you'll want to (or you can ask them to) **Label**, in a sentence, where they are now. This is very important to encapsulate all the feelings into a status. Examples may be "lost and uncomfortable in my own skin" or "ashamed of myself" or "treading water and not living up to my potential." If you state this, make sure they agree with that label. You'll get really good at this over time, and they'll get the sense that you know them better than they know themselves!

You'll bring back this one-sentence **Label** during the monster recap. For now, you'll transition into the next part, The Heaven. You can make a transition statement like:

"So enough about where you are right now… let's talk about where you want to be, and who you want to be, in 6 to 12 months…"

STEP 4: THE HEAVEN

Just like in the previous step, the goal in The Heaven is to make your clients *feel* the emotion (this time, in a positive way). Your prospect may just give you surface-level answers, and again, your job is to get them to visualize and experience their life without the bleeding neck issue.

Here are a few questions to ask:

"How are you going to feel in six months when you take action and gain back control over your health and fitness?"

"How is it going to feel when you _____ (paint the opposite of The Hell and get to The Heaven)?"

"Will it help you have more purpose in your life?/ How will you feel when you look in the mirror?/ Will you be happier?"

Next, you'll want to again (or ask them to) **Label**, in a sentence, where they want to be (or who they want to be). Examples may be "the sexy, confident woman I used to be" or "free of anxiety over how I look and feel" or "a man who is confident in his purpose and priorities." Like before, make sure they are in agreement with this **Label**.

STEP 5: THE MONSTER RECAP

This is where you bring it all together. Throughout the amazing process you've taken them through, they've likely learned quite a bit about themselves. Here's where you put it all together and qualify that they are ready to make the change:

> "This is where you are now _____ [insert Hell Label], and you want to be _____ [insert Heaven Label].
>
> It is 100% possible to make those changes and have that life but let me ask you this:
>
> Are you committed to change? Is this a priority for you? Are you coachable?"

Make sure there is urgency by asking, "Are you ready to do this?"

That's it for The Monster Recap. It's short, but it's powerful. When you sum up all their pain, hopes, and dreams so simply and succinctly, you build a huge amount of trust.

Now it's time to bring it home.

STEP 6: THE PITCH

The Pitch is what separates those who do well selling High-Ticket programs from those who become a Sales Jedi and can't help but sell this to nearly every lead they come in contact with—and see ridiculous, life-changing revenue and profitability spikes in their businesses.

The Pitch also takes the longest time to learn, refine, and master. It involves finding your own voice, and bringing your own emotion, your own "why," into play. It will take time for you to massage and refine this, and it will change and adapt as you get more adept at the Perfect Consultation.

Owen Daniels, as John Beckwith in the comedy *Wedding Crashers*, says, "You know how they say we only use ten percent of our brains? I think we only use ten percent of our hearts." When it comes to making our pitch, he's 100 percent right.

But once you find that sweet spot—once you connect with it and have 100 percent certainty and belief in it— you are unstoppable.

Some will find it in a few months, for others it will take a year. When you find it, you'll also become a Sales Jedi. Our PT Legends have benefited from getting in weekly reps over group Zoom calls. They've made their pitch live on the call with a small group of other gym owners. While it can be uncomfortable to pitch, especially around the veterans who are incredibly talented, you get good at it really quickly. But half the value is in hearing the pitches of other owners—you'll love the way Shannon phrased something, or you'll want to use a sentence or two from Matt's pitch and make it your own.

If you want to drop in on one of our calls to see how we create Sales Jedis, send us a quick email to salesjedi@ptlegends.com. We'll let you hop on and see what it's all about.

Your Pitch will be different depending on who you're in front of, and how your Perfect Consultation is going. It is vital that you know what you're going to prescribe to this prospect as the solution. You must be the Doctor. It's the certainty and belief that you have with what you are prescribing to the prospect that will sell your High-Ticket Transformation.

Let's look at three different scenarios:

Internal Drive Pitch: Your prospect has a bleeding neck issue and there is a strong emotional connection to making the change. They know they must do this, and are ready to make the change. A Hot Pitch will be made to someone who is looking for an internal change, not just an external change.

External Drive Pitch: Your prospect really wants to change, but the focus is more on the external change rather than the internal change. The bleeding neck issue isn't very painful. They're most interested in the weight loss or body composition change and not concerned with changing who they are.

Workouts-Only Pitch: Your prospect did not open up, you did not find a bleeding neck issue or make a connection, or they may only be interested in the workouts with no other goals.

INTERNAL DRIVE PITCHES

When someone is driven to make an internal as well as external change, they will recognize that this is the solution they most needed and didn't know existed. Barring a true affordability issue, they will be willing to spend the money even if it's outside of their budget.

Your goal is to not dig into the "how." Sell the vacation, not the flight! Keep them in the highly emotional state they are in—do not go into the details of your program. First, make your Monster Recap:

"Tammy, you came in here because you want to lose 25 pounds. But after talking with you today, and digging in deeper, I know this isn't about the weight. This is about the fact that you're living a life where you're just getting by—where you haven't made living your best life a priority for you. And where you want to be in six months—yes, you want to lose the 25 pounds and you want to lose the spare tire—but at the end of the day you want to wake up with purpose and drive to become the best mom, the best woman, the best person you can possibly be."

Then, get right into it. The Turn-Key Coaching System, and how you will take the guts of it, put your own spin on it, and make it your own, is freaking awesome. That being said—the person sitting across from you doesn't care. The only thing they care about is that we have the solution to their bleeding neck problem. So—do not get into the bells and whistles of the program (as exciting as they may be)! The pitch for someone looking for an internal change will be something like:

"Tammy, we created this program specifically for women exactly like you. It's a one-on-one mentorship program. We're going to bring you in here three times a week for workouts, we're going to customize your nutritional strategy, we're going to build the routines and habits, and create a mindset where you don't just lose the weight, but you wake up nine weeks from now and become the woman you were supposed to become."

Then, simply make your ask:

"Like I said Tammy, you are exactly the type of person we built this program for. The investment into the program is four thousand dollars, are you ready to do this?"

Your belief and certainty in the pitch will sell this. What you say is not as important is HOW you say it. If you are uneasy, and stammer at the price of the program, they will consciously or subconsciously pick up on that. You need to go in balls to the wall with conviction. If they trust that you can get them to the finish line, the sale is made.

There are many variations on how this pitch would go depending on how you choose to bolt-on your Transformation program. You may give them 2-3 options for your different programs and then ask which one they'd prefer to do. But for someone who is seeking an internal change, this is all you need to do to close it down!

EXTERNAL DRIVE PITCHES

You'll come across a reasonable amount of people who want to get in better shape, but their bleeding neck issue is wishy-washy. They would like to make some changes, but this doesn't seem to be a high priority for them—and it's focused solely on the external results.

For these prospects, you'll still do the Monster Recap, but when you pitch, you can describe a bit more of the program to gauge their interest.

You can tell them your "why"—the reason you created this Mentorship program. You can tie it in to the fact that you see people just like your prospect all the time, who gain and lose the same 10-15 over and over again, because they just start working out and possibly follow a short-term restrictive diet.

You can tell them you've built this program because you want people to create lasting habits and keep results for a lifetime. Be sure to personalize this and pull your story, or stories of people you've worked with, into it.

Then, you can expand on the components of your program. Here's an example:

> "There are 168 hours in a week. Working out for 3 of them won't change anything. Our program was built to take care of the other 165 hours in the week. Here's what we're going to do..."

> **The Workouts**: We teach you how to lift weights properly 3 times per week.

> **Daily Movement**: Enjoyable, daily activity to burn additional calories and make yourself a priority.

Nutrition: Your nutrition strategy needs to be customized so that you get to eat foods that you actually enjoy and still get results. We need to teach you how to eat and still enjoy life, not just follow a diet.

Routines: This is the most important part—and how we get everything to stick. We are going to build out your perfect day and perfect week, and hold you accountable to it until you change your habits and become the person you deserve to be.

Next, you can briefly show the Transformation Tracker and how you'll build this out and use it to change their habits. Tie it all together by letting them know that the most important part of the program is the weekly mentoring session—where we walk with you hand in hand through this journey, and lift you up when you stumble.

Confirm that they see the value in this program:

"Can you see how if you check the boxes every day for 63 days, after 9 weeks you'll become a completely different person?"

Then, get the commitment:

"Are you willing to put in the work? Are you willing to check off every single box for the next 63 days?"

From there, ask for the sale just as before.

WORKOUTS-ONLY PITCH

You are going to come across prospects who aren't a good fit for a High-Ticket Transformation program—and that's completely okay!

Remember, this is a bolt-on option. You still have all your regular services to offer afterwards. The brilliant thing about this is that with High-Ticket, you are price anchoring very, very high. If one of your traditional workout-only options is a better fit for them, you get to show them your High-Ticket offer, but then disqualify them and let them know that it isn't the best fit for them. You can then show them your regular options, and the prices will look that much lower. $180 to $600 per month looks a lot more reasonable when you were just looking at $4,000 and $6,000 offers!

There are three main reasons why your prospect won't be a good fit for a High-Ticket Transformation:

> **A. They are only interested in workouts and nothing else.** There isn't a bleeding neck or a desire to change at all—they just want to come in and have someone tell them what to do for workouts.

> **B. They aren't ready to change**. Some prospects will know they need to join your Transformation program and have a desire to, but they aren't ready to dive in this deep right now.

> **C. They truly cannot afford it**. They are 100% behind it and want to do it, but they truly cannot afford the program.

If you are closing scenario A, it's simple. You are still going to give the best Monster Recap that you can explain your High-Ticket Mentorship. Let them know why (with feeling, emotion, and passion!) this is the most important program that you have, and why it's important for you to bring this value to clients' lives, and how much of an impact it has. Let them know the cost of the program (price anchor), but immediately disqualify them.

> "Based off of our conversation today, it looks like you're here mainly for the workouts. Is that correct? Our Transformation Program is reserved for those who are really committing to a lifestyle change, so it wouldn't be the best fit for you. You are going to be a perfect candidate for _____."

Simply turn from your Transformation price sheet and show them your regular membership / training-only price sheet.

Pro-Tip: SIMPLIFY your existing price options. Do not have 6-12 different, confusing options. If you have too many, and it's too complicated, they are more likely to have to "think about it." Every business is different, but I recommend sticking to just group/semi/PT workout-only options here. If they want nutrition and accountability, they would be purchasing a Transformation program.

Because you've established authority and certainty in yourself and your services, and you've had an amazing, genuine conversation, and you've done the right thing by recommending a lower-priced program for your prospect, a workout-only option should be incredibly easy to sell at this point.

That's the beautiful thing about The Sales Resurrection System and selling a High-Ticket program—it's a truly bolt on program, and you should see an overall higher closing percentage no matter what.

If you encounter scenario B, don't go right for the Transformation sale. Potential clients may have a lot of things going on in their lives right now, and they aren't ready to make a lifestyle change. Or, they may know they truly need it, but they aren't mentally ready to face down their fears, rip off the Band-Aid, and go for it. They may not believe in themselves yet! Or, they may need more time to know, like, and trust you.

Whatever the case, don't let them walk away! First, give your Monster Recap. Pitch the Transformation program as normal, but let them know that you only accept people into this program who are truly ready to change.

"Based off of our conversation today, you see the value of this program, but you're not quite ready to go all-in. We're going to take action and get you started with _____ [down-sell option]. You'll make tremendous progress with this option and be well on your way to _____ [goal]. This will get you started and seeing amazing results. In 4 weeks, we'll sit down to review your progress and see if you'd be ready to take the next step. Sound good?"

Close the deal and make sure to set up that review session, a mini-Perfect Consultation, four weeks from the start date. By then, your clients will be feeling great about their progress, get to know the staff and the community, and have a longer period of time to know, like, and trust you. Many of our Legends are able to upgrade clients to High-Ticket in four weeks.

You'll handle Scenario C in a very similar manner. Get them going and have them take action by starting with a workout-only option (although we typically give them a starting plan to work with). Set up your follow-up Perfect Consultation four weeks into the future to see if they are ready for the next step.

Pro-Tip: Price will always be your biggest objection, but when you get really good at High-Ticket sales, you will be surprised at how many people will find a way to afford it (we're talking high-school kids, pizza delivery employees, etc.). However, when you do run into a price objection, make sure it is a true affordability issue before you downsell to a workout-only option. Do not drop your pants too early—it's a rookie mistake!

Then transition to a workout-only approach, but set a date for a future mini-Perfect Consultation to get an upsell to a Transformation Program down the line.

BUTTONING UP THE SALE

Once you get a "yes," make the awkwardness of getting the money as easy as possible.

> "I'm so excited that you're doing this. And I'm so excited that you found us! It's a perfect fit. I'm going to open up the calendar to look at a time to schedule your onboarding. Do me a favor and fill in your information here."

> [present them the program agreement with their name, contact information, and PAR-Q]

While they're filling out the form, I'll schedule their onboarding session, and then ask them:

> "You can use any card you want for payment. What would you like to use?"

By handing them the paper to fill out their information as soon as I get a commitment, I guarantee that they're in. Have your form ready to go and hand it to them with a pen.

However, your job is not finished. Buyer's remorse can set in, or they may go home and talk to their spouse, friend, or parents about the purchase. If they do, the average person is likely to think they're crazy for spending so much money on a fitness program. Then again, the average person is overweight or obese, living with comorbidities, and has awful priorities.

We've all had clients back out of a sale before. That can and will happen again. But you can take some preventative measures. Here are the four Tethering Steps:

> 1. Be *excited* for them. This is easy to do when you follow our processes, because you have such a deep connection with the person across from you. Let them know you are excited to be on this journey with them, and they are entering a new chapter in their lives.

> 2. Get them started *now*. Their journey begins today! Connect their personal Transformation Tracker (see Chapter 8) right away and have them set up their phone to put it on the home screen. Have them go home and fill out the Onboarding Homework today!

> 3. Book their Onboarding Session tomorrow. 48 hours later at the absolute latest. If you both have time after the consult, just get started right now! Don't let scheduling issues get in the way,

with your schedule or theirs. Everyone is used to Zoc now, so schedule the onboarding session over Zoom if in-pc. is not possible.

4. Send them a text to remind them of their Onboarding Home-work, your Onboarding Session date and time, and how excited you are to work with them.

We've all had sales that have backed out, and know how painful they can be. Implement these four steps to minimize the damage.

GET COMFORTABLE BEING UNCOMFORTABLE

The Perfect Consultation and The Sales Resurrection System is incredi-bly effective, but it isn't easy to learn or master.

You may have to go through quite a few Nos before you get your first yes. Expect your Nos to be more painful than your average rejection. It's not that big of a deal if someone doesn't join your 3x per week or unlimited CrossFit membership.

But, when you have an intense conversation with someone about the real issues, and there is much more on the line, getting a No hurts way worse.

Understand that this is normal. When you get several Nos, it may lead you to think that you aren't cut out for this, that you don't have what it takes. Everyone will go through this (even Dave Bess, the Kool-Aid man himself!).

The Nos just sting a lot more when you put yourself out there.

So be ready for it. Be ready for the rejection. It's part of the process.

In our PT Legends group, we celebrate the Nos. Every No is a step for-ward. Every No you get means you did your job. That you did the right thing even though it was tough.

With High-Ticket, the highs are incredibly high but the lows can be incredibly low. That's why our community of gym owners is so incredibly valuable. The encouragement gym owners give and receive to each other makes a huge difference. The community is what makes this fun. If you are a gym owner on your own island, you know how lonely it can feel and you know how painful it can be when it's just you at the helm.

High-Ticket sales is tough until it gets easy.

I know how hard it is when you ask for that first High-Ticket sale. You have an amazing conversation with someone you truly want to work with. You see how much they need this, and you know this program was built for someone exactly like this.

But, you're now at the point where you have to give them the price. You're afraid that you'll get that No—that they can't afford it or that you'll offend them with the price.

You start getting nervous and your hands are getting clammy. You're wondering if you can pull this off or not—then you start becoming self-conscious or looking or sounding nervous when you do tell them the price.

I always joke about this as the "butthole pucker"—when you get super nervous right before revealing the price and everything in your body is screaming to show them your old prices and forget the High-Ticket offer.

Do it anyways.

Growth comes when you choose to step outside of your comfort level. We have CrossFit gym owners who are doing this all over the world, in high-income areas and low-income areas.

If they can do it, why can't you?

They've changed their businesses, and their lives, and the lives of others, in ways they never thought possible.

If they can do it, you can too.

Now go get out there and get your first butthole pucker moment.

COREY WILLIS

Gym:

WILLIS KICKBOXING LLC

LOCATION: Billings, MT

IN BUSINESS FOR: 8 years

BEFORE PT LEGENDS & HIGH-TICKET:

I needed leads to produce more sales. More leads = more sales was my thinking. I always built up my sales by getting tons of leads and discounting a membership. I thought tons of clients was the key, but I was always spending time and money trying to get new leads. I also needed a ton of staff to train all these clients. It was a revolving cycle of bringing in clients, them not getting the big impact, and then doing another marketing scheme to bring in more clients. Exhausting. Plus I wasn't making a big impact on the majority of my clients.

AFTER PT LEGENDS & HIGH-TICKET:

In under eight weeks I upgraded twelve current members to my high-ticket Transformation Program and made over $20k in sales. My passion in helping others came back, and I love leading by example and seeing my high-ticket clients reach new levels they never thought they could.

AMAZING HIGHLIGHTS:

With the crazy market, I didn't need to get a ton of leads to make my gross sales go up. I added $20K without selling a membership. I was struggling to find leads for two reasons: 1) studio gyms like mine started coming in on every street corner in Billings and it saturated my market, making it very difficult to find leads. 2) Covid has changed the staffing in a way I can't really explain, but I can't find quality help to run my gyms effectively.

What I did was transform myself, made 1 or 2 posts about my progress and people wanted to know how I did it. Within 72 hours of learning the DC and PC, I sold my very first $3k No Excuses 63-Day Transformation. And in 8 weeks I sold 12.

I would be selling more if I wasn't tied up training 40 hours a week and trying to find qualified trainers for a majority of my time. Makes me rethink how I do business from here on out.

CHAPTER 8

THE TURN-KEY COACHING SYSTEM

"You know how they say we only use ten percent of our brains?
I think we only use ten percent of our hearts."
— John Beckwith, *Wedding Crashers*

Over the span of my career as a big-box personal trainer, department head of personal training, independent contractor, and gym owner, I've been exposed to my fair share of attempts to scale nutrition coaching.

I've tried multiple systems, and I've had some individual success with some of them. But the biggest problem I've had has been when I've attempted to scale this and teach other employees how to do it.

The coaching methods were either too complicated, or the employees felt they didn't have enough experience or knowledge to be confident.

It wasn't their fault; even I've felt out of my depth on occasion!

As fitness nerds, quite often we geek out too much on the technical details. We want to explain to our clients how our body metabolizes protein versus sugar and other information that is ridiculously unnecessary for your client to know.

More importantly, your client doesn't give a shit about the science lessons!

They just want the results. They want to solve their bleeding neck issue. So, your job is to keep the education to a minimum and focus on the specific actions they need to take instead.

That is what truly works. The Turn-Key Coaching System is the easiest, simplest, and most scalable system I've used over the past 14 years. And paradoxically, despite its simplicity, it is the most effective system I've ever used to create results.

The challenge was designing a system that is structured enough to ensure consistency in its execution, but flexible enough to work for all the different types of clients you'll need to work with.

It would also need to be method agnostic—meaning that it would need to allow for the use of any "diet" or method of tracking. In other words, it needs to work no matter what plan of attack you are taking with your client.

You also need the ability to see all of your summarized client data quickly, at one time, while also having the ability to quickly take notes and see what action items you previously assigned. Speed and simplicity is key here, particularly when you as the owner aren't doing all the work.

A strong, two-way connection across all platforms is invaluable—being able to access this from your phone or any computer, without having to fumble with logins or running into syncing errors.

It's the small, inconvenient things that crush compliance and cause either the client to bail on it, or the employee to not follow up or use it properly.

The art of success lies in simplicity.

Make sure your tools are as simple and easy to use as possible. It doesn't have to look incredibly sexy or have tons of features that look neat on the surface—chances are you'll never use them anyways.

THE ART OF COACHING

"Perfection is achieved not when there is nothing more to add,
but when there is nothing left to take away."
— *Antoine de Saint-Exupéry*

I could write an entire book on the art of becoming a fantastic nutrition, accountability, and motivational coach. And there are many courses already out there built by some amazing coaches.

While those will help you tremendously, you can get going right now. You don't have to spend $6,000 on a certification and spend precious hours memorizing the Krebs cycle. Your clients... DO. NOT. CARE.

To be clear, I am not discouraging you from continuing to learn and racking up advanced certifications. What I'm saying is that we tend to overcomplicate simple matters. There are many things to know about nutrition and the human body, but actual weight loss is very simple.

It's not what you know that is important in the art of coaching, it is how you apply it.

Bruce Lee has famously said, "Simplicity is the key to brilliance."

The art of coaching is rather simple, really. Spend less time on teaching them theory and science (they don't care), and more time on coaching them to take right action.

The heavy lifting has already been done with the Sales Resurrection System. You've had an amazing, genuine conversation and you've revealed to your client how big of a problem this bleeding neck issue is—and now they know what it will cost them if they don't take action.

This is so important, because it's the only way they'll be ready and motivated for real change. You'll soon see that a client who has gone through the Sales Resurrection System will be more motivated and malleable to change than any other client you've worked with.

This makes your coaching WAY easier.

So now your client is ready for real change. Now what?

Again—it's pretty simple. What does your client need to do, on a daily and weekly basis, to get to where they need to be? What key actions do they need to take to make it happen?

What does that day and week look like?

Typically, we'll have four main habits that we'll track. These are what work well for us and for our clients. The important thing is that you treat every client as an individual. It's easy to completely overwhelm clients with too much at one time. As you get better at coaching, you'll get a feel for what different clients are ready for.

Here are the main habits that are the most important to track:

Workouts: Duh. Typically, we have everyone work out 3 times per week. Yours will obviously be a CrossFit workout. 3 times per week is perfect for the average person.

Daily Movement: During other days, we often have clients take 15-30 minutes out of their day to move. This could be going for a hike, taking the dogs for a walk, playing basketball, or doing a quick yoga flow—whatever they are most likely to do and enjoy is typically the best choice. Yes, they're getting extra calorie burn in. But this is also a mindset exercise as much as it is a physical exercise. They are getting in the habit, with everything else going on in life—work, kids, activities, errands—to take a few minutes and make themselves a priority each day. To slow down, to shut off from the world, and to connect with themselves.

Nutrition Strategy: This is an obvious one. Typically, we want to focus on habit change and teaching them "how" to eat, not just follow a diet. We need to incorporate foods they enjoy eating to make this a long-term strategy. You can choose to take any number of routes for nutrition. For some, you may want a compliance tracking system like a Pick 1 Plan (pick a protein, pick a veggie, pick a carb, pick a fat), and have them track their breakfast, lunch, and dinner as a compliant/noncompliant meal. For others, you may have them log their food in a journal or app. For others taking baby steps, maybe you're starting as simple as drinking one soft drink a day instead of five. Your Nutrition Strategy should change and adapt over the weeks as your client masters the basics.

Routines and Structure: Structure is what helps your client stay compliant. Typically you'll choose one or two habits that will build structure into their day. One thing that helps universally is to have a plan for your nutrition the next day. Lack of planning is the reason why most people hit the drive-through. Another example of structure is a consistent bedtime. Many clients stay up late scrolling on their phone or watching just one more episode of Netflix. Irregular bedtimes create a lack of sleep—and this in turn affects energy levels and willpower the next day.

All you need to do is figure out the few things they need to do each day and week and hold them to it.

So how do you start?

The first thing you'll want to do is assign them homework. Interviewing them on their daily habits, how they currently eat, etc. takes valuable time. It's far better to have a form ready for them with the questions you need to know the answers to. You'll want to assign this right when you successfully close the Perfect Consultation; get them started on their journey ASAP to prevent buyer's remorse from setting in.

We connect our software to them right on the spot, and they can record all their answers. Here are some examples of data that will be useful to collect regarding the four main habits:

The Workouts

What days and times can work to schedule your workouts?

What injuries, limitations, or aches do you have?

Is there anything in particular you want to work on or emphasize?

Daily Movement

What activities do you enjoy? (treadmill, biking, hiking, yoga, walking the dog, swimming, sports/activities, etc.)

Nutrition

What do you eat for a typical breakfast, lunch, dinner, and snacks on an average weekday? Weekend? What are some variations?

When are you hungriest?

How many times a week do you eat out or get takeout?

How many times a week do you eat a meal that you're not in charge of / do not prepare?

What liquid calories do you consume (coffee, tea, smoothies/protein shakes, soft drinks, energy drinks)?

When you go on binges, what foods do you eat? How much?

What are your weaknesses with snacks? How much do you eat?

What does your pantry/freezer/fridge look like?

Do you do any type of meal prep? Do you plan out meals in advance?

Who prepares the meals in your household?

Is your family going to do this with you? Would you like them to?

Do you like to cook or would you prefer to just warm up pre-prepared stuff foods?

Have you ever tracked calories? If so, what app did you lose?

Are you open to tracking calories for the next 9 weeks? (hint: people who do this see the best results)

Routine/Structure:

What time do you wake up? Is it a regular time? Is it a different time on weekends?

Are you tired when you wake up? How long does it take you to get going in the morning?

What does your overall daily schedule look like? Please write out your schedule (work, family, activities, etc.)

How much time do you spend on TV/Internet/Social Media each day? What does your screen time say on your phone?

What time do you get in bed?

What time do you fall asleep by? How many hours of sleep do you get on average?

What activities add joy or meaning to your life that you no longer do or don't do enough?

What habits could you start that would improve or add greater meaning or purpose to your life?

What habits do you have now that aren't serving you in a positive way or are holding you back?

At the same time you assign this homework (when you close the Perfect Consultation), you'll also book your Onboarding Session.

THE ONBOARDING SESSION

During the Onboarding Session, you'll review their answers, and ask follow-up questions that will help you determine what habits to choose. It's important that this is an open dialogue—you can't just tell them what their daily life should look like and expect them to do it.

You'll need to offer them choices, and help steer them in the right direction. Make sure they are really bought in. You can ask, "Is this something that you realistically can do every day? Are you willing, and can you commit to doing this every day?"

If you can't get a firm commitment, if they're not enthusiastic about it, you're setting them up for failure. You'll need to keep asking questions and you'll need to offer different solutions until you make that connection.

Once you've determined what you'll be tracking, you'll want to build out their Transformation Tracker. Now, you can just use pen and paper, but I would suggest making this electronic across any platform—laptop and mobile.

The reason is two-fold:

Number 1, for the clients. Clients will baulk at tracking with the slightest bit of inconvenience. They aren't going to carry a notebook or piece of paper everywhere they go. Even if it's in a different room in the same house they'll use that as an excuse not to track. But you can count on their phone being within arm's reach every minute of their lives. So, make sure access to the Transformation Tracker is on the home screen of their phone!

Number 2, for your employees and ease of scaling. If your clients are using pen and paper, you can safely bet on them "forgetting" to bring this at least half the time. You'll never have consistency, which is the only thing that matters for results. In addition, the Transformation Tracker eliminates the need for your coach to create and maintain separate notes on your client and prescribed action items (let's face it—most of your employees are not that organized and are not great at keeping records). If you're using a Transformation Tracker similar to what we use, everything you need is in ONE PLACE (the onboarding homework, the tracker, additional nutrition tools and guides, and renewal/retention/review section—more on that later). Your coach will record notes every week in the same tracker—for measurements, wins and struggles, and action items. Nothing will get lost! And best of all, you as the owner can check at a glance if the work is actually being done!

For our PT Legends clients, we provide all the tools for our gym owner clients, so you have everything that you need, and you can private-label and customize the tools with your business and brand.

But to get started right away, you can easily create one in Google Sheets. DO NOT get hung up and spend loads of time building something out. Remember: your clients don't give a shit about how pretty your tools are. They don't care "how." They just want to solve their bleeding neck issue and create an identity shift.

Here's an example of a starting Transformation Tracker:

TRANSFORMATION TRACKER

THE 63 DAY TRANSFORMATION

Start Date: _____

MY REASONS WHY
1. _____
2. _____
3. _____

MY 9 WEEK GOALS
1. _____
2. _____
3. _____

WEEK 1	Sun	Mon	Tue	Wed	Thu	Fri	Sat	ACTUAL	GOAL	%	Week Review
☐ Meal 1: Pick 1 Plan	☐	☐	☐	☐	☐	☐	☐	0	7	0%	Measurements:
☐ Meal 2: Pick 1 Plan	☐	☐	☐	☐	☐	☐	☐	0	7	0%	_____
☐ Meal 3: Pick 1 Plan	☐	☐	☐	☐	☐	☐	☐	0	6	0%	_____
● Snack: 200 Calories Or Less	☐	☐	☐	☐	☐	☐	☐	0	6	0%	_____
🏋 Workout	☐	☐	☐	☐	☐	☐	☐	0	3	0%	What went well this week?
✔ Move For 15-30 Minutes	☐	☐	☐	☐	☐	☐	☐	0	4	0%	_____
✔ Track Today/Plan Tomorrow	☐	☐	☐	☐	☐	☐	☐	0	7	0%	What did I struggle with this week?
◎ Routine 2	☐	☐	☐	☐	☐	☐	☐	0	5	0%	_____
WEEK TOTAL								0	45	0%	Coach's Notes:

ACTION ITEMS
1. _____
2. _____
3. _____

It's pretty simple. You choose the habits you want them to track and how many times per week they need to do it.

After you build out their perfect day and week, all you need to do is schedule their weekly, recurring coaching/mentoring call.

While you can certainly do this in person, it's typically better over a Zoom or video call. It's more convenient, easier to schedule, and can be done anywhere. As an added plus, when we get into The Flawless Renewal System, you can get an amazing video testimonial by recording the call. If you have multiple locations, or plan to, you can also have one employee who provides the coaching/mentoring for multiple locations.

The Weekly Mentoring Call

Your weekly calls are typically 15-20 minutes, maybe a bit longer for your first two or three. They are incredibly simple to execute in four steps:

1. Review the data. Take a look at the numbers: the percent compliance and any measurements you are choosing to track (weight, body fat percentage, waist measurements, etc.).

2. Celebrate what went well this week. Most of the people we work with will just focus on what went wrong, or where they screwed up. We need to make it a practice to celebrate all the small gains they've made. Call out and praise them on what they're doing well.

3. Identify where they struggled. Where did they struggle the most? Was it snacking at night? Was it poor planning over the weekend? Have a good discussion around this. Ask probing questions and identify solutions and ways that you can make this easier in their lives.

4. Give them one key action item for next week. Typically, this key action item will be help reduce the friction with whatever they're struggling with.

Depending on how your clients execute, you may need to adjust their habits from time to time. They may be overwhelmed, and you may need to reduce the frequency of certain habits or eliminate them altogether. Or, they may be crushing it and ready to stack on an additional habit. Perhaps there is another habit you can add that makes all others easier or even unnecessary.

The point is, you'll be modifying their perfect day and week as you adjust it to their real-life circumstances. That's how you'll gradually shift their habits over time to creating a lifestyle change.

TRANSFORMATION TRACKER

THE 63 DAY TRANSFORMATION

Start Date: March 19, 2022

MY REASONS WHY
1. I want to be comfortable in my own skin again
2. I want to have my confidence back
3. I want to feel sexy again

MY 9 WEEK GOALS
1. Establish consistent nutrition habits
2. Lose 12 pounds
3. Run 1 mile without stopping

WEEK 1	Sun	Mon	Tue	Wed	Thu	Fri	Sat	ACTUAL	GOAL	%	Week Review
#1 Meal 1: Pick 1 Plan								7	7	100%	**Measurements:**
#1 Meal 2: Pick 1 Plan								5	7	71%	156 lbs
#1 Meal 3: Pick 1 Plan								6	6	100%	29.5 abdomen
Snack: 200 Calories Or Less								4	6	67%	
											What went well this week?
Workout								3	3	100%	Feels way more motivated and energetic
Move For 15-30 Minutes								4	4	100%	Breakfast is 100% locked in and easy
											What did I struggle with this week?
Track Today/Plan Tomorrow								7	7	100%	Late night snacking was tough
In Bed By 10pm								5	5	100%	Tend to get cravings and overeat
WEEK TOTAL								**41**	**45**	**91%**	**Coach's Notes:**

Coach's Notes:
Awesome first week. Repeated weeks like these
will result in 1-2 lbs/wk of fat loss
Snack (dessert) will be right after dinner. After,
you'll brush teeth immediately to discourage more

ACTION ITEMS
1. Track every day this week, #1, 2, and 3 priority!!!
2.
3.

That's it. It's ridiculously simple. If you approach this mentoring call with high energy, encouragement, and keep it action-oriented, you'll have an amazing amount of fun and success.

Have empathy, but keep your Doctor Frame! And don't take any bullshit answers or excuses. Be assertive as well as supportive, and keep them in the bumper lanes.

When they're hitting a rough spot, sometimes you need to bring back their 3-5 real reasons why they absolutely need to make this change in their lives. Reconnecting with their "whys" should help bring back the motivation that naturally declines over time. That's also why they need to continuously celebrate their small wins and gains week after week.

Obviously, there is much more you can learn to master being an amazing mentor. But you have to start somewhere. You have to get going first. The reps and experience will help you more than anything else. Start by doing, then increase your learning as you go along. That's precisely why we hold weekly trainings on coaching and fulfillment. You simply can't learn everything from a book—no matter how big it is.

There is a big difference between theory and action. Go take action!

LAUREN DERVELOY

Gym:

CROSSFIT RUSTON

LOCATION: Ruston, LA

IN BUSINESS FOR: 9 years

BEFORE PT LEGENDS & HIGH-TICKET:

I didn't know my worth and value. I was charging way too little for way too much work. I was burning the candle at both ends and felt imprisoned by my business.

AFTER PT LEGENDS & HIGH-TICKET:

Oh wow. PT legends has changed our entire trajectory as a company. Made all of our investment back after being in PT legends for 3 weeks. We are financially free and paying our staff more than we've ever been able to. We can breathe and actually enjoy life.

AMAZING HIGHLIGHTS:

$19,500k in new business sold in my first month.

HIGH TICKET FOR AFFILIATE GYMS

CHAPTER 9
THE FLAWLESS RENEWAL SYSTEM

"Those who say it can't be done are usually interrupted by others doing it."
— *James Baldwin*

Particularly in the CrossFit space, our High-Ticket has not been without criticism. The leading criticism is actually a speculation.

A year ago, when critics scoffed at the success PT Legends gym owners began having with High-Ticket programs, they would say:

"Sure, the high-ticket thing is nice, but what about retention? There is no data on how this works long-term. How many people are really going to pay these rates long-term?"

Well, the data is in, folks, and it looks f-ing amazing. The long-term effectiveness of High-Ticket is not up for debate anymore. It is proven and the math speaks for itself.

Our top Legends are CrossFit gym owners. And they're seeing renewal rates of 80% for Transformation programs, and 90-100% if you include downgrades to group or personal training only options.

The first 2-3 months on your profit and loss statements are great when you add High-Ticket Transformations- you can bring in an extra $5,000, $10,000, even over $30,000 in a month. But it's a whole different story when the renewals come in and you're adding those in with the new business.

Many of our Legends typically hit all-time revenue records in the first 2-3 months only to blow them away in another month or two.

But let's not forget that the speculative argument—"But what about retention?"—may not even matter for some of you in the first place. How many months does your average new member stay? And what is their average monthly spend?

Quite often, the average lifetime value of a new client is less than even one Transformation sale. I've seen many gym owners that would mathematically be ahead with High-Ticket even if renewals were at zero percent.

That being said, the power of High-Ticket isn't in marginally increasing your revenue and profit. The power of High-Ticket is that you can radically change your profitability incredibly quickly. For your average CrossFit gym, selling just two Transformations programs a month, with decent retention, will result in you taking home an extra $50,000 to $100,000 this year!

Renewals are incredibly important. It took us a while to iron out how to perfect this system. It will also take you some time to master it. When you do, the data shows that you will see a higher retention and renewal rate for your High-Ticket programs than you will for your regular memberships.

So, let's dive in and look at how The Flawless Renewal System will help you not only with retention, but also with the all-important reviews and referrals.

THE 6-WEEK STORY

Have you or one of your employees ever waited until the last session of a package, or the last day of a membership, to ask for a renewal?

I've been guilty of this rookie mistake many, many times over. Sometimes it was due to poor organization and not knowing when the memberships were up; other times, it was because I was fearful of hearing a "no."

When you wait until the last day or week, you're really setting yourself up for failure. You either

A) give them a super-easy way to tell you "no" ("I have some trips coming up. I'll just take a quick break and let you know when I'm ready to come back"), or

B) look like you have absolutely no plan for what's next for them—devaluing your services and giving them less of a reason to want or need to renew.

Don't make this rookie mistake.

You're going to have this renewal conversation at the end of week 6 (if your Transformation program is a 9-week program like mine is).

Why have it so early, you ask? We as human beings have a very short attention span. Our interest levels wane over time. What was once new and shiny becomes old and dull.

Even the best of coaches will see motivation and excitement come and go. By week 6, your clients have had enough time to see some amazing changes, both physical and mental. They are feeling the benefits of having more energy and having better habits—and now the scale, and how they look, is also starting to really show.

It's during this period of high excitement that you want to have the renewal conversation. The way we initiate this is by first assigning our clients homework at the end of week 5. They're instructed to fill out this homework prior to their mentoring call at the end of week 6.

We build this directly into the same Transformation Tracker that we use to build and record their perfect day and week. As a gym owner, don't you hate patching together 6-8 different pieces of software, forms, etc? The more complicated something is, the lower the chance it will be executed with consistency.

So keep it simple! The Transformation Tracker is where you should on-board, track, coach and keep notes, have any nutritional or educational information that is needed, collect your reviews and referrals, and perform your renewals.

The homework for our clients is put in a section called "Week 6 Reflection." For us as business owners, Reviews, Referrals, and Renewals are all-important. We can get those from our clients—but let's spin it for their benefit as well.

We ask them questions about their story, their impact, and their growth.

Their "Story" becomes our Review.

Their "Impact" becomes our Referral.

And their "Growth" becomes our Renewal.

Here's an example of how it can be laid out:

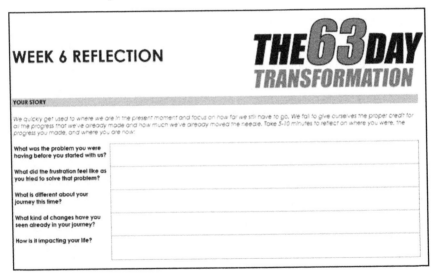

Because we've assigned this as homework, the good news is that they've had to time to think and reflect on their journey—and to process how they are changing as a person (not just on the scale). And because it's done digitally, this amazing journey can easily be copied and pasted into a Yelp, Google My Business, or Facebook review.

YOUR STORY (OUR REVIEW / TESTIMONIAL)

Here are some questions to ask that will get you amazing reviews and set you up for easy renewals:

What was the problem you were having before you started with us?

What did the frustration feel like as you tried to solve that problem?

What is different about your journey this time?

What kind of changes have you seen already in your journey?

How is it impacting your life?

YOUR GROWTH (OUR RENEWALS)

With the questions above, you already have them thinking about how they've changed over the last six weeks. Now, this is where you ask them to think about "what's next for me?"

Ask:

"It's important to never stop growing, and always looking to level up. Take 5 minutes to think about what's next for you after your initial 9 weeks. What do you want to work on next?"

We'll give them prompts and short-answer fill-in-the- blanks for:

Goal 1

Goal 2

Goal 3

Habits I want to start

Habits I want to stop or change

YOUR IMPACT (OUR REFERRALS)

This is where we'll get our referrals. Now, there are advanced ways to get referrals by putting an amazing offer in here for any friend/family member. If you have an irresistible free offer that doesn't give away the farm, put it in here.

If not, don't worry. Just stick to something like this:

> "You may not be aware of it, but you are the source of inspiration and encouragement to someone else who needs a helping hand to get started on their own journey. Sharing your transformation has the power to change someone's life that you care about. What family member, friend, co-worker, or even someone in a group you belong to can we extend an invitation to? Note: it's okay if they aren't local to the area!"

It's important to let them know it's okay if they aren't local. Why? Because many of your clients have a sister, best friend, or parent in another state who desperately needs this Transformation. And the beautiful thing is: you can still help them virtually. Remember—the workouts are overrated. You can send them the workouts to do on their own. It's the mentorship that makes the difference. We sell our virtual programs at the same price as our in-house programs. You can too!

THE 6-WEEK REFLECTION MENTORING SESSION

By assigning them to do the homework, half of your job for getting the renewal is done. Make sure to check in with them so that it's completed!

This is a great session to record; it will make an amazing testimonial video. If you're doing this in person, ask ahead if they'd be open to you recording their story to inspire others. Just use your phone to record the entire session. If you're doing it over Zoom, it's even easier.

When you have your mentoring call at week 6, BRING THE HEAT! Make it a very high energy, high value conversation. Perform your regular call, then review the Week 6 Reflection.

Ask them the same questions in the "Your Story" section and let them tell you about their journey. Ask probing questions to expand on who they are becoming, not just the results they are seeing. Do some digging to bring out the emotion. Then, add one final question to the end:

"What would you say to someone who's on the fence about starting this program?"

Their answer should be 100% gold for a testimonial video!

After they finish, give a monster recap of where they were before, and where they are now. Then say:

"This is amazing! Look how far you've come in just six *weeks*. Imagine where you'll be when you keep this going in six *months!* Twelve months?!"

Then you can ask them what they want to work on in the next phase of their journey, after the nine weeks.

From there, you just name the price of continuing with your mentorship options and make that renewal happen seamlessly. After you handle the renewal, you can then get the referral.

RENEWAL OPTIONS

Remember, adding a High-Ticket Transformational offer to your existing CrossFit doesn't necessitate you changing your business model. It's a complete bolt-on. We typically help you customize your back-end, or renewal offer to best fit your business, your specific challenges, and your location demographics.

That being said, there are a couple of different options on how you can construct your back-end offers.

You can offer the same 9-week program at the same price, and a reduction in price if they commit to 6 or 12 months. You can choose to bill the same way as they previously paid (PIF, 2-pay, 3-pay, etc.)

You can keep everything at the same price, but offer a "light" package that has a mentorship call one or two times per month instead of weekly.

You could also offer a "light" package where the mentorship call is done in a group setting. This has massive potential as it scales very well, and has a massive impact in retention as it builds more connection and community.

Clients may feel like they have such an amazing structure built where they no longer need the mentorship. This is great, too! Convert them to a training-only PT or group membership and keep them going. If they ever slip in the future, pull them back into a mentorship.

In some cases, you'll have clients who were willing to pony up and pay the High-Ticket price initially. They still see the value, but it is truly something they cannot afford on an ongoing basis. That's great as well— move them to a "light" or PT / group only program and keep them moving forward.

You should see a much higher renewal rate from your High-Ticket clients than just an average person coming in for a group membership.

PRE-FRAMING THE JOURNEY

If you want to take your renewals to the next level, you're going to take what you now know, and apply it way back in the sales process.

You can do this in the Perfect Consultation or the Onboarding Session—but make sure it's one of the two.

Explain to clients that their true journey is a 6-12 month process. You'll need to make this language your own and learn to refine it, but here's an example of how you can pre-frame this journey:

> "In the first nine weeks, we're going to focus on building a solid foundation. We're going to build the key habits that will provide structure in your daily life and set you up for long-term success. The end-level results you're looking for will take longer—around 6-12 months. Depending on how you do in the first nine weeks, we'll figure out what options would be best for you afterwards. But, we'll have to see how well you execute. After 5-6 weeks, we'll sit down and figure out what plan would be best for you."

What I'm doing here is really just framing that this isn't a 9-week journey—that the nine weeks is only the first step of a much larger journey. And I'm also letting them know that we'll be sitting down to talk about renewal options. There is no surprise, there is no awkwardness. Remember: you are the Doctor. This is your proven process that changes lives.

There are other advanced ways you can spice this up. To encourage clients to really get off to a fast start, and to even get them to qualify to continue with a High-Ticket mentorship option, you can let them know that:

> "depending on how you do, I may potentially invite you into my Alumni program. I extend this to only those who are really

committed to change and do an amazing job, so we'll have to see how you do first…"

By doing this, you can get them extremely motivated to be very compliant right out of the gates, and they will actually try even harder to be invited to renew with you.

That being said, don't try to put all of these techniques into play right at first. It will be overwhelming. Get some reps in and get comfortable selling first before you worry about adding a pre-frame.

KEEPING YOUR DREAM CLIENTS

Remember, the 6-Week Reflection is a sales opportunity. Treat it just like a consultation. It's even more valuable—this is someone who already knows you, trusts you, and has already given you thousands of dollars. Don't mail this session in—treat it like the golden opportunity that it is to land a brand new client!

Once your dream client tells you how much their life has changed since starting this journey with you, and they tell you what they would say to someone who's on the fence about starting the program ("You *have* to do it! It'll be the best decision you ever made!"), it's very difficult for them to say they'd like to discontinue.

You're the Doctor—go in with the belief, certainty, and conviction that they need from you to continue on with the next phase in their journey.

Take their written story and have them copy and paste it for reviews. Take their video testimonial and use that for your content marketing. And take their referral recommendation and make an offer for a 7-Minute Discovery Call.

When you get great at The Flawless Renewal System, you'll find that the pressure to always need new business starts to fade. And when your

High-Ticket base starts to grow, that's when you really reach an entirely new level of revenue and profit with your business.

FEATURED LEGEND

ANDREW FREZZA

Gym:

FITTOWN JUPITER

LOCATION: Jupiter, FL

IN BUSINESS FOR: 9.5 years

BEFORE PT LEGENDS & HIGH-TICKET:

Our biggest obstacle was not being able to serve people in a deep way who needed more from us and were willing to pay for it. We would do a decent job in our sales process, but then undersell and under-deliver on what people needed from us. This made us feel like we were always chasing the next person to grow our business.

AFTER PT LEGENDS & HIGH-TICKET:

The added revenue has helped us get through a tough time in our business, and gave us confidence that we can withstand any future unforeseen circumstances. In many ways it has renewed my love of coaching and helping people, knowing the deep impact we are capable of with any single individual.

AMAZING HIGHLIGHTS:

I think the biggest thing is how quickly we were able to make our first sale, and pay off the cost of the PT Legends program. Since we've started, we've "only" brought in $25,000 in additional revenue through PT Legends, but we've implemented a small portion of it so far. As our team continues to grow, this number will be a drop in the bucket compared to what we will bring in the future.

CHAPTER 10
HOW TO GET STARTED

"Two roads diverged in a wood, and I—
I took the one less traveled by,
and that has made all the difference."
— Robert Frost

This shit works.

It works so exceptionally well that it completely changed my life as a gym owner in a matter of a few short months.

Reading this book is the easy part. But taking action and implementing the strategies is challenging and uncomfortable at times. It's going to require that you level up. So first, let's get clear on why it is your obligation to bolt on and execute a High-Ticket Transformation program into your gym—why it's important for you to have high prices.

You owe this to yourself. You have taken on a huge risk as a gym owner. If you do not make a good living in return, it isn't worth it. Without high enough margins, there isn't enough money in the bank to hire cleaners, or companies to handle your ads, or trainers and coaches so you can move on and focus on growth. And if you burn out, everyone suffers. The ability for you to have an impact in your community dwindles.

You owe it to your family. They deserve to have financial security and to have the best opportunities you can provide to them. They also deserve your time—to spend with them and be fully present, not stressed about if a coach will show up, whether or not someone will renew, or if you're saving enough money for a vacation or retirement.

You owe it to your staff. Let's face it: as owners we all feel a responsibility to provide a great job to our employees. We want to be able to provide them steady work and good pay where they can make this a career. With standard market prices, there just isn't enough money to do this. The margins aren't high enough; the math doesn't check out. You owe it to your staff to provide a means for them to make a good living.

Finally, you owe it to your clients. Changing lives is NOT easy. No matter how good your fulfillment is, if it's only a few hundred bucks a month, your clients will think, "Sure, I'll give it a shot." But if you're charging $3,000, you have their full, undivided attention. They *are* going to make the change, they *are* all-in, and they *will* change their lives.

Everyone wins when you charge premium rates. The only question is whether or not you have the stones to do it.

Sara Carter, a CrossFit gym owner in Gulfport, Mississippi started with us last year in 2021. After finishing her year-end taxes just a month ago, she discovered she made $100,000 more than she did the previous year (income, not profit!), after working with bolting on a High-Ticket offer with PT Legends—and she didn't even start until May!

If you are worried that High-Ticket won't work in your small town or city with lower-income demographics, try looking up Gulfport, Mississippi and seeing how your area compares:

Census.gov Income & Poverty Statistics (2016-2020):

Median household income: $40,554

Per capita income in past 12 months: $23,907

Persons in poverty: 23.7%

In her own words, Sara sells $2,000 Transformation programs "like Skittles." Her Transformation program is 3x/wk group, 1 Onboarding Session, and 1 weekly Mentoring Session. That's it!

As her group expenses are a fixed cost, I'll let you do the math on the margins for that one!

Her Transformation programs delivered as personal training are $4,500, and she and her staff sell them on a regular basis.

If Sara and her staff can do this in Gulfport, Mississippi, this can be done *anywhere*.

You *can* do this.

You *need* to do this.

It is your *obligation* to do this—for yourself, your family, your employees, and your clients.

THE GUARANTEED ROUTE TO SUCCESS

Let me just be completely transparent with this.

If you want to absolutely crush it by bolting on a High-Ticket Transformation program and make an extra $100,000 this year, you need to work with me and the team at PT Legends.

While the techniques in this book are simple and massively effective, most of you reading this book will fail to put them into action and have the confidence to work through your missteps and figure it out.

I've given you absolute GOLD in this book. The techniques we've covered in these chapters are worth one-hundred grand without a doubt. While there is no way I can cover everything in this book (it would easily be over 1,000 pages), I also haven't held anything back.

But—**information isn't enough**!

Think about all the friends or family members that asked you to build them a program for them to do on their own. Because you care about them, you took the time to build and write out their entire exercise and nutrition plan in detail.

How many of them actually saw results? A whopping zero percent.

If information was enough, you'd be out of business.

The success rate of people who go at it alone is dismally low. The highest achievers on the planet all have coaches. Tiger Woods needs a coach. So does Russell Brunson, Lady GaGa, and Bedros Keuilian.

But maybe you're thinking you're the exception. And maybe you are!

So why would you still consider investing good money to work with me at PT Legends?

Jason Cohen with Locomotion Fitness has the answer. When we began talking about working together, he said, "Oh, I know I'm going to get something going for this. The question is if I need your help to do this. And please don't take that the wrong way!"

I love when people are blatantly honest. My response to him was, "You are smart enough to figure this out on your own. That being said, we'll put you four to five years ahead of schedule and have you closing at 20 percentage points higher than you ever would on your own. AND we'll train your staff for you."

Thankfully, Jason is smart enough to know that you pay for shortcuts. And in his first eight weeks, he sold $40,000 in new business (even while he lost his salesperson and was on vacation for two weeks!), making his ROI almost comically ridiculous.

And while his results are amazing, they are also not uncommon. Many, many Legends have sold over $20,000 and $30,000 in their first four weeks of execution. But yes, some only sell $5,000 to $10,000 as well. That being said, for CrossFit gym owners, even selling "only" 1-2 of these a month will likely be your best month ever for new business!

There is a reason why we make absolute Killers in PT Legends.

It's because you get to talk to us, and have live trainings where you're getting in reps, five days per week!

There is no other mentoring system that can touch this.

You're getting on calls with us, practicing your craft and honing your pitch, live with us in a small group, week after week until you become a Sales Jedi.

There are some things you just can't learn from a book. You can read books on boxing all you want, but if you get in the ring without hands-on training you're going to get your ass kicked.

Confidence, finding your own voice, personalizing your pitch, handling objections, and becoming a Sales Jedi takes reps, practice, a teacher, and a community.

That's what we do. That's why we produce Killers in 12 weeks who change the entire trajectory of their business and lives.

That's my pitch. I don't want to shy away from it. You can make your money back in as little as two sales. It's about as no-brainer as it gets.

If you are committed to making at least $100,000 more this year, book a call now at: https://www.ptlegends.com/bookacall

Of course, we offer much more than just this. As you would expect, you'll be getting access to the latest marketing ads, copy, and landing pages that are working, help with operations, business development, and more.

But if you are resolved to try this on your own, take action today!

You know how to do a Discovery Call, right? Perfect—start there! When your next lead comes in, send them the text message and hop on the phone.

No matter what, don't read this book and say to yourself, "This is great. I can see how this can completely change my life. I should do this sometime once I… [have some time / solve my staffing issue / figure out where I'm going with my business / solve my lead program]."

If you waited until the perfect time to make big changes in your life, you'd never get them done.

Perfect timing is a myth. You just need to take action.

You have so much to gain by adding a High-Ticket Offer to your services. You have absolutely nothing to lose.

Is it scary and uncomfortable? For most of you, yes. But that's where the growth and excitement in life is—beyond your level of comfort.

I'll leave you with the immortal words of Theodore Roosevelt from his Paris, France speech on April 23rd, 1910, an excerpt known as "The Man In The Arena":

"It is not the critic who counts; not the man who points out how the strong man stumbles, or where the doer of deeds could have done them better. The credit belongs to the man who is actually in the arena, whose face is marred by dust and sweat and blood; who strives valiantly; who errs, who comes short again and again, because there is no effort without error and shortcoming; but who does actually strive to do the deeds; who knows great enthusiasms, the great devotions; who spends himself in a worthy cause; who at the best knows in the end the triumph of high achievement, and who at the worst, if he fails, at least fails while daring greatly, so that his place shall never be with those cold and timid souls who neither know victory nor defeat."

Life is too damn short to hold back.

Start today. You got this.

ANDREW ROMEO

Gym:

ROMEO ATHLETICS

LOCATION: Enfield, CT

IN BUSINESS FOR: 13 years

BEFORE PT LEGENDS & HIGH-TICKET:

The confidence to sell a mentoring service. Then the confidence to know how to sell this service. Realizing your value and being able to charge for it is priceless.

AFTER PT LEGENDS & HIGH-TICKET:

We have a much higher close rate all together, specifically with our higher priced options. Less clients, higher prices, equals a better product and more enjoyable company to run.

AMAZING HIGHLIGHTS:

20% revenue increase in Q1 2022 over Q1 2021.

Hourly rate of $750/hour to work on mentoring.

I'm opening my second location because of the knowledge gained from PT Legends.

BONUS CHAPTER:

SELLING HIGH-TICKET TRANSFORMATIONS TO YOUR EXISTING CLIENT BASE

*"You have $20,000 to $100,000 in High-Ticket revenue
just sitting there in your gym right now."*
— Dave Bess, the "Kool-Aid Man"

The great thing about having a High-Ticket offer is that you don't have to change your business model.

It's simply another offer—the best offer—for those who need more than just workouts. When you bolt your High-Ticket offer onto your front-end sales process, the results are staggering. Your average sale will skyrocket, and your overall closing percentage should improve with the high price anchor.

But our most successful Legends who have CrossFit gyms are also selling Transformation programs to their existing members and bringing in tens of thousands of dollars in new business simply by having a few conversations.

One of our PT Legends, operating a franchise fitness kickboxing gym, sold 11 Transformation programs, all on the back-end to his existing clients, in his first month working with us (well over $20,000!). And his members are only paying $99/month! If Corey can do this, there is no reason you cannot.

THE SIMPLE FACT OF THE MATTER IS THAT PEOPLE NEED MORE THAN WORKOUTS.

It is your job to provide the solution to their needs.

Every single CrossFit owner reading this book can think of 5-10 existing members who would be a perfect fit for a Transformation program. In fact, right now, take a sheet of paper and write down the first names that pop into your head—names of people who *need* this program.

Actually do it. Put down the book and write these names down. I'll show you a quick play that can run to make $10,000 this week.

THE $10K IN 5 DAYS PLAY

Do you have your list of 5-10 members? Perfect. Here's what to do next:

Ask them, "How have you been doing lately?" It's best if you can do this in person, but you can also do it over a text conversation or at a goal review. The overall goal is to have a bit of a Discovery Call with this conversation.

Sometimes, your members will be in a tough place. They'll be struggling with stress, family, work, eating, or weight loss/gain. If they open up about "The Hell," and you establish they are ready to change this, simply let them know that you built a mentorship program designed to put them back in the driver's seat. Then, offer a Perfect Consultation.

> "Sorry to hear that you're struggling with all of that. I know how hard that can be, and how much that can weigh on you mentally as well as physically.
>
> But I'm glad that you're ready to tackle it head on! Let's set up a time to sit down and game plan where you need to go from here

and what you should be focusing on. If you're really ready to take the next step, we built a mentorship program that solves [their exact problem]. You may potentially be a good fit for it, but if not we still need to build an action plan for you."

From here, set up a mini-Perfect Consultation with your existing member. Don't forget to assign the "whys" for their homework as well!

If your member doesn't open up right away with some sort of pain or problem, do some digging. Asking questions like—"Are you happy with your progress?", "How far are you from your goal weight?", or, "When you came in here you wanted to do x, y, z. Are those still priorities for you?"— can open up the conversation.

Keep in mind that most fitness professionals are scared to ask these questions—because if their clients aren't seeing great results, they worry that it's a poor reflection on their abilities as fitness professionals.

But remember, you are The Doctor. Doctors don't feel personal responsibility for their patients' conditions if they prescribed a medication to solve an ailment and the client didn't take it, correct?

But, they may feel responsible if they didn't prescribe the right solution for their patient.

If your client is seeing results because they are just working out and nothing else, they *need* more. Have the confidence and the certainty to tell them exactly this. Tell them that this is exactly why you designed your mentorship program. Prescribe what they really need. Show them that they have a bleeding neck issue, what will happen if they don't take care of it, and exactly what they need to do to fix it.

If you need additional help upgrading your existing clientele into a high-ticket Transformation program, feel free to email me scott@ptlegends.com and we can put together a bespoke solution for you.

DAVE BESS

Gym:

UNDERGROUND FITNESS

LOCATION: Glendale, AZ

IN BUSINESS FOR: 6 years

BEFORE PT LEGENDS & HIGH-TICKET:

Biggest obstacle was false beliefs and knowing there wasn't something more than just counting reps and assigning macros. We hit a $40K ceiling and could never get past it.

AFTER PT LEGENDS & HIGH-TICKET:

My clients are absolutely changing from the inside out. We are guiding and leading real transformations now. I have more time to spend with my young son and amazing wife, and I have real purpose to my day. I feel I can really make an impact in the world.

AMAZING HIGHLIGHTS:

Sold $45,000 in High Ticket Programs during a 30-day sprint.

Sold a $10K 9-week Executive Program.

ADDITIONAL RESOURCES:

My Email: Gym owners are my tribe. I would *love* to hear from you and welcome any questions, feedback, or even hate mail that you'd like to send to me.

scott@ptlegends.com

Tips, Tools, & Future Books: Would you like to be updated with free tips, tools, and future book launches? Stay tuned for future books on objection handling, advanced sales, and nutrition coaching. You can get these delivered to your inbox if you get on my mailing list:

www.coachscottcarpenter.com

The PT Legends Podcast: My weekly podcast show to help gym owners succeed in all aspects of business and financial freedom:

Apple and Spotify links at www.ptlegends.com

The PT Legends Facebook Group: Dave and I regularly post free resources and live trainings for High-Ticket in this group, and it is a place for you to meet and learn from other gym owners implementing High-Ticket:

https://www.ptlegends.com/freegroup

Book A Call: Would you like to hop on a quick call to learn more about working with me to help you bolt-on, sell, and fulfill a High-Ticket Program with your specific business model? You can pick out an open time here:

https://www.ptlegends.com/bookacall

Recommended Books: I am a big reader. Leaders are readers and earners and learners. While there are many books I could recommend, the following is a short list of books that could be considered complimentary, whether obvious or not, to you leveling up and becoming a High-Ticket Coach, sharing your gifts with the world, and living a life full of purpose and abundance:

Who Not How by Dan Sullivan & Dr. Benjamin Hardy

Atomic Habits by James Clear

Do The Work by Steven Pressfield

The Obstacle Is The Way by Ryan Holiday

Killing Sacred Cows by Garrett B. Gunderson

Switch by Dan & Chip Heath

Expert Secrets by Russell Brunson

The 12 Week Year by Brian P. Moran & Michael Lennington

The Gap And The Gain by Dan Sullivan & Dr. Benjamin Hardy

Extreme Ownership by Jocko Willink

The One Thing by Gary Keller & Jay Papasan

Traction by Gino Wickman

Good To Great by Jim Collins

The Perfect Day Formula by Craig Ballantyne

ACKNOWLEDGEMENTS

I used to romanticize the idea of being a self-made man. But as I learned from my hero, Arnold Schwarzenegger, the idea of the self-made man is a myth.

There are many, many people to whom I owe a debt of gratitude for the development of this book and the strategies contained within.

To Dave Bess, who was instrumental in the creation of our High-Ticket strategies and the best sales trainer in the world at PT Legends.

To Ron Edward, without whom my gyms would have likely collapsed during my darkest times as a gym owner.

To Clayton Bonaguidi and Shane Nichols, who along with Dave and Ron first championed our techniques and proved their scalability in Underground Fitness.

To our OG Legends—the ones who asked me to teach them how to implement this in their fitness businesses, and forced us to build a business around it. Your contributions to the program and the PT Legends Community have made it 10x greater than it otherwise would be. Thank you, Laken Summerville, Deonte Mason, David Oquendo, Colm O'Reilly, Derek Davis, Sara Carter, Matt Chenard, Shannon Logan, Taryn Dubreil, Lauren Derveloy, Jennifer Dawson, Jeff Larsh, Dan Visentin.

To all the amazing Legends thereafter and the amazing contributions you've made to the program.

To Scott Rammage and Josh Price, amazing men and business owners, and our first and biggest supporters.

To all the mentors and coaches I've invested in, worked with, and learned from over the years.

To my parents, who instilled in me a strong work ethic at an early age.

To my wife Nicole, for tempering my rough edges and helping me become a better and more complete man.

To my sons Maddox and Finley, for inspiring me to do my best.

Thank you all.

Made in the USA
Monee, IL
12 June 2023

35685410R00096